WHEN THE CASSEROLES ARE GONE

THE FAITH COMMUNITY'S RESPONSE TO GRIEF

Guides to Practical Ministry, #7

Energion Publications
Gonzalez, Florida
2023

The Poem "Lament Psalm 5" on pages 71-72 is from Ann Weems, *Psalms of Lament,* (Louisville, KY, John Knox Press, 1995), p.9, and is used by permission, all rights reserved.

The section Tricks Your Brain Plays on you During Grief on pages 73-77 is by Dr. Bob Baugher, PhD, and is used with his kind permission.

Figure 1 on page 45 is reprinted by permission of the publisher (Taylor & Francis Ltd, http://www.tandfonline.com), with publication data shown in the footnote at that location.

ISBN: 978-1-63199-864-5
eISBN: 978-1-63199-865-2
Library of Congress Control Number: 2023935365

Energion Publications
P. O. Box 841
Gonzalez, FL 32560

energion.com
pubs@energion.com

TABLE OF CONTENTS

SERIES PREFACE

Once clergy leave seminary, they quickly discover there is more involved in congregational ministry than they learned in school. They may have touched upon many issues faced by clergy in their practical ministry and preaching classes, but there is always more to learn. An internship may have allowed a person to get their feet wet, but again there is much more to learn. As important as this foundational education is (and I believe seminary is important), experienced clergy quickly discover that much that goes into pastoral ministry must be learned on the job. Once a person enters congregational ministry, they quickly discover their strengths and weaknesses. Therefore, continuing education and regular reading in the field are essential. Clergy must have access to books and articles written by experienced clergy *for* clergy.

The Guides to Practical Ministry book series was originally published in partnership with the Academy of Parish Clergy. While the APC has brought its more than fifty-year existence as a professional association for clergy to a close, Energion Publications is committed to continuing this series as a legacy of the Academy of Parish Clergy. This series is designed to provide clergy with resources written by practitioners—that is by people who have significant experience in local congregational ministry. Some of the authors in this series have spent time in academic settings, but they all know what it means to serve a local congregation.

The books that appear in this series cover a variety of issues and concerns faced by clergy. Books in the series address such areas of concern as writing sermons, serving in interim ministry, engaging in ministry in the community, engaging in clergy self-care, clergy ethics, administrative tasks, the use of social media, worship leadership, and pastoral care to name a few. Because most clergy are generalists and not specialists, they need to develop a variety of skills. Sunday morning might involve preaching a sermon while the next day, or even later in the day, they might be sitting with a parishioner who is dying or meeting with a family planning a funeral. With these books, we hope to contribute to clergy growth in congregational ministry.

Congregational ministry can be a rewarding vocation, but it's not an easy one. While these books are designed to assist clergy in becoming effective in ministry, the legacy of the Academy of Parish Clergy, is a call to collegiality. So, perhaps these books will be best used in conversation with other clergy so that together they might share the practice of ministry.

On behalf of Energion Publications, I pray that the books in this series will be a blessing to the authors who writer these books, the clergy who read them, and all who share in or receive ministry from the clergy who read these books.

Robert D. Cornwall, Ph.D.
General Editor

AUTHOR'S PREFACE

This book begins at the end. Literally. It begins with the call that says someone closely connected to a faith community has died. There has been an ending to a life. That call comes because the faith community is needed. People who are members or have a history with a specific church, synagogue, or other faith community, know that this is what you are supposed to do. You call someone at the church because you know that they are going to help. This is the group that can put together and provide the support so desperately needed at such a time.

The primary discussion here, however, begins after the call has gone out, the obituary has appeared in the newspaper, and the sad news has been told on social media sites. This book is about what happens after the funeral or memorial service is over and the after-funeral luncheon or reception has ended, and everyone has cleaned up the fellowship hall and gone home. What happens next? That is the central question I have been pondering and now am attempting to answer, at least in part, through this book. What is the role of the faith community in the life of a grieving individual or family the days, weeks, and even months after a death?

In these pages, you will find the outline or foundational structure of a process for attempting to meet the needs of bereaved persons in your faith community. It includes suggested timelines, information about setting up a Bereavement Team, and information about the nature and journey of grief. The Appendices offer further resources that can provide training information and guidance.

A principal premise of all of this is the central truth that grief does not go away. Ever. Mourning generally gets less intense and life-consuming, but grief itself does not end. Those who suffer a significant loss do not walk through grief as one might endure a miry bog or an uphill climb, knowing that it is tough but that you will put it behind you after a bit. Rather, when a loss occurs, grief comes to journey with us for as long as there is a single memory or story left to share. That's the way it should be. We are beings created for relationships and the result of being in a relationship with another person, or loving another individual, will be grief if we live long enough to say goodbye.

The faith community is often involved in the life of a person and family when an individual is dying. The faith community is generally involved in the funeral or celebration of their life. The faith community provides the initial support of the family or loved ones. Should it not be the faith community that also joins them in their journey with grief rather than leaving them to traverse the challenging and sometimes demanding path by themselves?

It has been my intent to make this discussion ecumenical and interfaith. For that reason, I have chosen the term "faith community" to describe any church, congregation, or other groups that meet around a common faith purpose and ideal. There are times I have used the words "church" and "congregation" for ease of description, but everything written here is for whoever can find in it, a direction for ministering in a new way to those who grieve.

All names used in stories told here are not the real names of the persons represented, and in a few circumstances, they have been altered enough to retain anonymity where it is warranted.

I want to thank my spouse, Jamie, who has helped with proofreading the manuscript and asking potent questions such as, "Is this really what you mean to say?" I also want to acknowledge our adult children, Amber and Corey. When I was early in chaplaincy and, at the same time, still serving full-time as a parish pastor, they often did not have very much of me around and ended up taking an undeserved back seat. Much of my early experience and education around end-of-life issues came at their sacrifice.

Thank you also to an old college and seminary friend, Dr. Robert Cornwall who, when I asked for advice about publishing a book, offered to serve as editor of this volume and connected me with his publisher. I also owe gratitude to the staff of hospitals and hospice organizations with whom I worked. They trusted me and encouraged me, even when I bothered them with the "there are no stupid questions" stupid questions as they taught me about healthcare, life, and death.

Certainly, so much of what is here and so much more has come from parishioners, hospital and hospice patients, and their families. I tried to learn from the "human document" that was before me. Sometimes I was not a real quick learner, but I was educated in life, death, and bereavement by wonderful and gracious teachers while they lived and died through difficult circumstances and allowed me to be a fellow traveler on their journey.

CHAPTER 1 — WHO DIED?

Casseroles, as far as one-dish meals are concerned, can be the center of a hearty meal. They are portable and they feed a lot of people while accounting for who knows how many nutritional categories, all in a few bites.

When serving as a parish pastor, I had the opportunity to taste many, many casseroles. Some were outstanding. Some merely accounted for nutritional needs, and some were, shall we say, not worth the energy consumed in their creation. Casseroles made an appearance when it was time for one of those ever-present after-church potlucks or picnics. A good excuse for missing the worship service was to volunteer to remain in the kitchen, rotating the casseroles in and out of the oven so that they would be warm after the final "Amen."

Casseroles of every possible concoction also made significant appearances when a church member died. Sometimes the casseroles were intended for the luncheon reception served right after the funeral or memorial service. Other times, these one-dish meals or other consumables were taken to the home of the bereaved to help feed the family members coming into town for the funeral. They were also presented to take the burden of cooking away from grief-stricken individuals.

When our two children were young and saw a casserole go into the oven early in the day or when they saw desserts or salads under construction that were large enough to feed a crowd, the standard question that came out of their mouths was always, "Who died?"

It was very clear to any Preacher's Kid that the food wasn't destined for the family table, so the logical, and usually correct conclusion was that somebody in the congregation had died.

It is only natural that this very caring, traditional, and ancient method for conveying condolence should be shared with a grieving family or community that has experienced a loss. That is true for a couple of different reasons. The first reason is that we use food and drink to say that we care. It is what we do. Never mind the fact that grieving individuals often don't much feel like eating in the hours or even the days following a significant tragedy or death. They will need food in the house, and, after all, "you should eat something." The fact there is food in the house gives them the opportunity to just pick at a little something or eat a meal as they choose.

The second very practical reason for taking food to a grieving family is that you know you should go to them and say something, and it is easier to go with a purpose beyond just knocking on their door and saying you are sorry for their loss. It is easier to arrive at the door, food in hand, as a reason for the visit. It works out great. It avoids the question of whether you are supposed to hug the person because, after all, you have a hot dish in your hands. Casseroles and desserts also come with built-in dialogue about what's under the aluminum foil covering, how easy it was to fix, how to warm it up and how it can be served. There is no need to come up with words to express something for which there are no words. Don't misunderstand me, words are generally always appreciated and usually appropriate. As we will discuss later in this book, the less said with the maximum authenticity of caring is what is best. Standing there with a slightly tipped hot dish in your hands and hot gravy running down your wrist somewhat relieves that natural and immediate need to come up with how to start the dialogue.

Someone we know has died. Someone is now sad, bereaved of the life and relationship that has been irrevocably wrenched out of one's grasp. It is right and traditional that the community reaches out to offer solace and assistance. And so, we take a casserole, side dish, or dessert. There will likely be a funeral with a luncheon or reception of some sort following. The church, school, or neighborhood phone tree starts rolling and you are asked what dish you would like to bring.

I am not suggesting that casseroles are bad or that we should not provide food in response to a death. Family members will be making a journey and it is important that the bereaved family whose home will likely serve as grief headquarters not be overly burdened to purchase and prepare mass quantities of food. Throw in a box full of paper plates and cups, plasticware, toilet paper, and a can of coffee, and caring is multiplied by practicality.

As for the after-funeral dinner, this is a long-held and time-honored tradition in many cultures. It is much more than a chance to sit and visit or trade recipes ("Who brought that triple fudge chocolate cake? I have to have that recipe!"). The meal is symbolic of the continuation of life that goes on despite the loss of death and the grief it leaves in its wake.

I know one person who feels that it is quite "barbaric" to sit down to a meal or share food and the table fellowship that occurs right after a funeral. She believes that people should leave the funeral in quiet contemplation and introspection, remembering the deceased in their own ways. I attempted to persuade her that the meal, the conversation, and the shared memories, far from barbarism, are affirmations of life that continue despite and in the face of death. Casseroles after a death can be good and any dessert that involves coconut is even better.

Traditions and customs around food and eating at a time of death and bereavement can be found through time and cultures.

The ancient Celtics held very elaborate funeral ceremonies with gatherings of clan members. These gatherings included large banquets. The deceased was sometimes buried with food and other items needed by them in the Otherworld.[1]

---

1   Lynne Ann DeSpelder and Albert Lee Strickland, *The Last Dance: Encountering Death and Dying*, 7th edition, (New York, NY, McGraw Hill, 1998), pp. 120-121.

Traditional native Hawaiian customs called for a feast or full meal following the funeral. Then there was another feast to mark the one-year anniversary of the death known as '*aha'aina waimaka* or "Feast of Tears" which was a reunion, of sorts, of those who had shared their tears before.[2]

Sharing of food is very prominent in traditional Jewish faith practices. While the funeral is happening, there are people in the family home preparing the *Se'udat Havra'ah* or "Meal of Consolation." In the seven days following the funeral, the family sits *Shiva*. During these days normal life for the family is interrupted. Some do not go to work, there is no shopping, and there is to be no meal preparation by family members. The needs of the family are provided for by extended family and by friends.[3]

Whether it is food brought to the home in the hands of caring friends or casseroles brought to the church kitchen for a funeral reception, they are gifts of community. Food acknowledges the need of people, not just to eat, but to be together in their grief and their memories. It brings community to the grieving individuals or families that might otherwise find themselves isolated in their grief.

A definite change in practice and custom has impacted this long-held tradition. As more and more people, at least in the Western United States, prefer cremation over full body burial, it means that the memorial service can be delayed until it is a convenient time for family to gather. That may be a few days, weeks, or even months after the actual death. In the days of the COVID-19 pandemic, some services were delayed by as much as a year or more. It is possible that there would not be a reception that needs food brought in. If and when services are held long after the death has occurred, it seems to inspire fewer people to attend. Most people, by that time, have moved on with life and prefer to continue in that direction. This doesn't, however, lessen the need for food to be

---

2   DeSpelder and Stickland, *Last Dance*, pp. 82, 345.
3   Judith Houptman, "Death and Mourning: A Time for Weeping, A Time for Healing, in *Death and Bereavement Around the World,* Vol. 1. Morgan and Laungani, eds., (Amityville, NY, Baywood Publishing, 2002), p 63.

provided in the home to free grief-stricken family members from the chores of figuring out menus and cooking meals. That remains an important outreach that close friends and members of a faith community can provide after a death.

So, a person has died, and people are needing their community to respond. The food is consumed after the funeral or in the home in the days surrounding the death. Then what? If the food and meals provided represent the community and the communal sense of grief and empathy with the family and closest friends, what happens next? What occurs when all the shared food has been consumed or frozen for later? What do we do once the 9x13 glass pans and the Bundt cake pans have been washed and returned to the homes from whence they came? If the first question in the pastor's home is "Who died?" Then the next question asked in the days following is what happens when the casseroles are gone?

The remainder of this book is an effort to answer that question, particularly for faith communities who are wondering that very thing and seeking ways to help the bereaved in their community of faith. We will look at the nature of grief and then some very concrete steps that can be put in place by faith communities of any size. The gift of food is important in those early days after a loss. The grief of those bereft of a loved one, however, far outlasts the casseroles and three-bean salads. The gifts of the church to those who grieve can be gifts of genuine hope and comfort for the weeks and months to come.

CHAPTER 2 — EMPTY DISHES

Having enough food available after there has been a death in the faith community is rarely a problem. Food is taken directly to the home of mourners and food is provided for the meal following the funeral. When that meal ends, the leftovers generally go home with the family. Eventually, the food has been consumed, which means many empty dishes must be taken back and reclaimed. There are often the ever-present leftover containers made of empty margarine tubs or whipped topping bowls. Those often become the "mystery bowls" in the refrigerator. When I was a child, you were never sure whether it was margarine or leftovers in those plastic dishes. If you thought it was margarine and it was indeed leftovers, it likely had turned fuzzy by the time someone opened it.

Eventually, the Jell-O salad, dessert, and casserole dishes come back to the church to await their reclamation by the rightful owners. There is often some guesswork involved in this endeavor since almost all 9x13 baking dishes look pretty much alike. Some cooks will have applied the obligatory piece of masking tape with their name on the bottom of the dish in the hope that it wouldn't come off when it was washed. The identification serves two purposes. First of all, it helps the dish find its way back to the owner right away rather than having to let it sit until everyone else picks up their nearly identical dishes. The one left must be yours. Secondly, identification on the dish allows people to know which home chef to contact ("that dessert was amazing," "who made that casserole," or "I have to have your recipe").

This presents its own problem, however, since this dish has already been shared within the faith community and the recipe has made the rounds. Therefore, the cook can't bring that same dish to another church function without changing churches.

When everyone has been fed, family members from out of town have all gone home and all the dishes have been returned to their rightful owners, there are those left behind who are still feeling very, very empty. They came to the table and maybe they ate or maybe they couldn't. These are the ones nearest to the deceased and there is a big, cavernous feeling inside of them that even Mrs. Martin's famous Dutch apple pie can't fill.

Life moves on as the lives and experiences of people who were close at hand shortly after the death return to whatever their normal might be. They can't remain always in the place they were or in the role that they filled at the time of death and the time of the family's greatest need. Nor should they. For most of us, the world keeps turning, even if it seems to have stopped for a woman who lost her husband or for the parents who have lost a child.

The emptiness one feels has a name and it is grief. Grief doesn't end because the tuna casserole has been consumed, the dish washed and returned to the church kitchen. "But we had the funeral and even the luncheon." "All the casseroles are gone, and the tables in the Fellowship Hall have been wiped down." Now the people who provided this wonderful, necessary, and loving service are going on with life. It isn't that people don't still care or still have hearts that ache for the bereaved. It is just that not everyone can continue to live life with the same level of grief and mourning as those closest to the deceased will experience.

A woman who was a member of a grief group likened her experience with grief as if she were hiking with a group of friends. Starting on the hike, they were all together. No one goes too far ahead, and no one gets left behind. But as time goes on, some of the people begin to move more quickly and the distance between the bereaved woman and her supporters begins to widen. Pretty soon, as her grief journey continued, she felt like she was walking by herself and everyone else was way ahead. She could still see them, and she could hear them as they called for her to hurry and catch up. "What's keeping you? Come on, walk faster." And so, she described her feeling of being left behind, unable to walk any faster while watching her supporters moving away over the hilltop in the distance.

This is normal and to be expected on one level or another. If it is perceived that everyone who cares for the bereaved has moved too far ahead, however, it can leave a person who has just experienced an earth-shattering death, wondering what is wrong with them and why they aren't moving forward. It can lead to feelings of abandonment on one hand or a sense that they shouldn't bring up their grief or the deceased's name out of the concern of being a bother to others who have their own lives to live. Sometimes it can be a matter of having no safe and welcoming space to talk about such things.

People who try to be helpful are sometimes less than that. When you grieve and someone tells you that they are worried for you or are praying for you, it can leave you feeling like something is wrong with you or with your particular way of grieving. Platitudes don't help much either. One thing that I share with people after they have experienced an especially tragic or young death is to know that people want to help, they want to say the right thing, and they want to make your grief go away. In those efforts, many will share some comments that are anything but helpful and, in fact, can be quite hurtful. People want to tell you how they or someone they know coped with grief and how you should do the same thing. They will offer something they have heard that they feel is appropriate even though it is not. We've heard them all: "God needed your child more than you do;" "God needed another flower for heaven's garden;" "you can always have more children;" "they are in a better place so you should be thankful;" "they lived a long life;" "I know just how you feel;" and on and on it can go.

We need to cut a little slack to most all but the most egregious of comments ("Thank God you have other children to love"). Likely, these people have yet to experience a significant death in their lives and are doing the best they can to try and make you feel better because they assume that there actually are words that can accomplish that after a significant loss.

These platitudes and comments, however, serve to do little other than shut down any significant conversation the bereaved might want or need to have. And, believe me, people who have suffered a loss really do want to talk about it, but only with people open and willing to hear them. Too often they have opened up to someone about their grief only to be told that they shouldn't feel "that way," or they've been made to feel that they are just plain weird for feeling or behaving the way they do.

Former Oregon Governor, Barbara Roberts talks about this in her book where she describes her journey through her husband's illness, death, and her own grief.

"I have a hundred secrets about grieving. Some people may think my secrets are strange. I do not tell my secrets about grieving to anyone because they might think my secrets are too weird. How do I know they are weird? Because I have heard these judgments about grief and how it is supposed to work hundreds of times throughout my life. And so I have a hundred secrets. My secrets are about trying to cope with the huge hole in my life where my husband and others I have loved and lost used to be."[4]

The reality of grief is that you don't get over it. Grief doesn't end. It changes and sometimes eventually becomes easier to live with and to live within but as long as there is a memory left to hold, grief doesn't totally go away. There is nothing friends can do and nothing that a faith community can do to make grief disappear. Friends and family can be supportive; they can be helpful, but they can't fix it. Grief doesn't need to be fixed and grief can't be fixed. Grief becomes part of us as it touches our soul and heart. Some

---

4   Barbara Roberts, *Death Without Denial Grief Without Apology: A Guide for Facing Death and Loss,* (Troutdale, OR: New Sage Press, 2002), p. 75.

days our grief will be easy to live with and less noticeable. On other days it can bring us to our knees without reason or prior notice.

One of the best descriptions of this came from a young woman in a grief support group. She was grieving the loss of her sister. She told us that there were times when she could get through her day with little grief-related intrusion. On other days, she could be going through her normal activities when she would suddenly get hit in the head with a "sad stick".

Grief isn't something that can be wished, hoped, or prayed away. But that doesn't mean that those who grieve should be left alone with the dark hole of loss that leaves them feeling sad and very alone. While there are many places these days where people might reach out for support in their grief, there is one place that would seem the most natural and important. That is the local faith community of which the griever is a part. The faith community was there when they needed an officiant and supporters for the funeral or memorial service. When they needed food to feed members of their family or to serve a group after the service, the faith community was all-hands-on-deck.

But when the casseroles are gone and when the dishes have all been emptied, washed, and returned, how will the grief be acknowledged? Who will be there to understand the nature of grief and to provide the support that is so desperately needed but so many are unwilling to seek out? When all we do best is done and over with, then what? More casseroles are not going to cut it now. It requires people who are available and knowledgeable to open doors to allow grief to be welcomed into a place of assurance and hope. It takes a village. It takes a community. In many cases that community is already formed as a faith community and needs only to understand the depths and soul of grief and how to be present as a listening and supportive community.

CHAPTER 3 — THE CHURCH RESPONDS

Most faith communities with whom I have been associated have considered themselves to be warm and welcoming communities. The desire to be friendly and hospitable is sincere. This is even more so if the visitors are a family bringing children or adolescents with them. After all, such visitors just might give a sense of purpose to the newly hired Youth Pastor who is supposed to single-handedly attract this often-absent population and thus save a maturing congregation from looming atrophy.

There may be greeters at the doors to welcome visitors and even congregants assigned to sit with newcomers in worship. This gives visitors someone to talk with and as well as a veteran worshipper to help them understand the order of service and liturgical choreography (kneel, stand, go forward, or stay put for communion, when to smile, and shake hands, etc.). After the service, there will be an invitation to the coffee hour where everyone is encouraged to be friendly and accommodating to guests.

When it comes to members or visitors who have experienced a recent loss, it may be a very different scenario during worship services or any other gathering of the faith community. Nothing can put a damper on a good church picnic like someone talking about how life has changed for them since the death of their spouse. A person in a worship service can easily find themselves alone when they tend to break down in tears when certain hymns are sung.

Most pastors can relate to planning worship services while avoiding certain hymns that were sung at the recent funeral of a church member. This is an effort to make sure family members, or the congregation are not made uncomfortable by an emotional recollection.

It isn't that people in the faith community don't care or are unaware of the grief. They do see, and they are aware of how difficult it must be for the bereaved person. More than likely, they would like to help but they hesitate out of fear of saying or doing the wrong thing. While some people find contact with grieving persons quite comfortable, most do not. People may believe that giving a grieving person some space is part of being respectful and sensitive. What that sometimes feels like to the bereaved, however, is that people are uncomfortable being around them or talking to them. A person who was once active in a faith community can now be left feeling like a leper ("Unclean! Unclean! My husband died and I grieve. I'm unclean!").

The woman mentioned in chapter 2 who envisioned everyone moving on ahead of her and calling out to her to catch up, also spoke of what it was like to attend congregational functions. Her reason for no longer attending was that, although the church had initially been very supportive, "life moved on for everyone else and nobody mentioned it again. When they did mention it, they referred to Brad (her deceased husband) as 'your husband.' They all knew him well but after he died no one used his name. Even the pastor hasn't used his name since the funeral almost a year ago. It's like they have forgotten him. It makes me feel so lonely."

Let's face it. The idea of death and direct contact with persons who are grieving a significant loss makes many people feel less than comfortable. We live in a death-denying culture. Even the faith communities are not immune from the refusal to see the reality of death and the grief that follows. Famous anthropologist, Margaret Mead is quoted as saying, "When a person is born, we rejoice, and when they are married, we jubilate, but when they die, we try to pretend that nothing has happened."[5]

Grief can be hard to watch and difficult to be near. Part of that is the uncomfortable feeling of watching the pain of another, especially when there is little or nothing, we can do to mitigate the pain. Most people are much better at fixing people and making things right than they are at being in the presence of deep emotional pain. My daughter rightfully called me out on this when she phoned from several states away during her freshman year in college. She was upset by a couple of things and was crying on the phone and I, being the all-wise pastoral counselor, was trying to fix it and make her feel better. She finally brought me up short by saying, "Dad, I just need someone to listen to me cry." Megan Divine writes: "Grief no more needs a solution than love needs a solution. We cannot 'triumph' over death, or loss, or grief. They are immovable elements of being alive. If we continue to come at them as though they are problems to be solved, we'll never get solace or comfort in our deepest pain."[6]

Another reason that being near grief or grievers can be difficult is that it can easily lead us down a difficult path strewn with memories of losses that we have experienced. Sorrow often begets sorrow and grief can beget a grief that we would rather not have to experience again. In such cases, it is not the sadness of the grieving person that bothers us so much as our own wounds and reminders of loss sometimes still healing just below the surface.

There are times the newly bereaved are avoided because they might ask us questions that are difficult, if not impossible, to answer. The death of someone near to us, especially in tragic circumstances, can lead to questions about life, God, the role of God in our lives and in the death of our loved one, as well as questions about faith itself. The bereaved are trying to right a world that has been turned

---

5 Margaret Mead, (n.d.). *AZQuotes.com*. Retrieved June 28, 2022, from AZQuotes.com.

6 Megan Devine, *It's OK That You're Not OK: Meeting Grief and Loss in a Culture That Doesn't Understand,* (Boulder, CO: Sounds True, 1917), p. 59.

upside down by death or other loss. The image of what the world is and will be for them has been shattered and they desperately want to put it back together. A man who was once very active in the church stopped attending after the death of his son while his wife remained active. When asked about his absence he said that he wouldn't come back because no one had been able "to tell me why God chose to allow my son to die of painful cancer." Despite the fact that trying to answer this question is a no-win proposition, no matter what one says, it remains a cry from the depth of the soul that seeks desperately to understand the unfairness of the universe as well as life and death itself.

The death of someone close can, at times, challenge our faith on many different levels. While some may have their faith shaken by the death or the circumstances of the death, there are others who struggle with how their faith can seem to be wanting when they experience grief. We all live our lives in a self-made reality that is sometimes referred to as an "assumptive world." This world is an image, even an illusion, of what life is, what life for me is supposed to be, and what life will be for me and those I love in the future. It can also include my view of the Divine and how God works in this world and my life. In my assumptive world, "Not only do things make sense cognitively, but these things matter to us. Not only is the world understandable and manageable, but it is worth caring about and investing energy in."[7]

Death shatters the assumptive world that seemed so under-standable and manageable before the death occurred. Nothing is right with the world after a death. My present is missing what was once a part of me, and my future looks nothing like the future that I assumed would be there for me. What is left is the past, which, while comforting, does not do much to make up for the loss of a person in our present and future life. All our assumptions of what life is and should be are now damaged and rearranged.

---

7   Irene Landsman, "Crisis of Meaning in Trauma and Loss," in *Loss of the Assumptive World: A Theory of Traumatic Loss*, Jeffrey Kauffman, ed., (New York, NY: Brunner-Routledge, 2002).

There are times when people that could be supportive are not because the loss is not fully recognized. If the loss is not recognized, there should not have to be grief. This has come to be called disenfranchised grief. There are many losses that the public or those around the bereaved do not acknowledge as legitimate losses. Disenfranchised grief includes things such as miscarriage, stillbirth, death of an ex-spouse, death of someone who is elderly and has been ill for a long time, suicide, pet loss, loss of employment, moving away from friends and family, and other such losses. These and many others can be listed, and we will look at some in more detail later.

When the loss is not recognized, often the grief of the person experiencing the loss is not recognized as real or legitimate grief. This can be where well-meaning people may say things that are sometimes hurtful or seemingly uncaring. "Well, at least you didn't have the chance to get to know and love your baby." "You can always get pregnant again soon." "They were old and sick and are in a much better place now." "You've been divorced for a lot of years. I don't understand why you are even sad." "She was only a dog. You can get another."

All these and other reasons can keep very caring people of faith from providing support for those in their community who are grieving. It isn't only laypersons who may have a hard time responding to loss and subsequent grief. A community survey and study by the Missoula Demonstration Project: Quality at Life's End published in 2004 revealed that only 29 percent of faith community members felt as if their faith community provided adequate support for families at the time of death. In the same survey, one-third of faith community leaders and clergy told surveyors that they had received no training in areas of end-of-life, death, funerals, or bereavement.[8]

Since that time, I am hopeful that more recent attention to end-of-life and bereavement needs and issues would reveal better

---

8   Kaye Norris, Gretchen Strohmaier, Charles Asp, Ira Byock, "Spiritual Care at the End of Life," Health *Progress,* (July-August 2004).

results if the same survey was conducted today. Evidence of such change on a large scale is hard to come by. Hopefully, more recent research and writing in the areas of dying, death, and grief are making their way into the seminary programs and the continuing education of clergy and other professional faith community leaders. Let it also be noted that, as a young pastor, I did not have a lot of confidence in myself to do much by way of bereavement ministry or follow-up, short of occasional conversations with bereaved folks before or after worship or occasional home visits.

This book is based on the premise that grief is a marathon, not a sprint, and that the long-term care of grieving persons cannot be adequately met by only a pastor or other single faith leader. Even a well-trained and caring pastor needs assistance with the grief support of bereaved members. This is especially true in large congregations and aging congregations. Not only does this take some of the burden of appropriate bereavement follow-up off of the shoulders of the leader but it also assures that the bereaved person feels that the community has responded to their need. "After all", they may reason, "it's the role of the pastor to help me through my grief." But to have other members of the community reach out, especially if they are trained appropriately, can help someone feel more support and realize that the larger community of faith is aware of their needs and willing to meet them where they are.

While it is hoped that there will be specific leaders of the congregation trained to be grief support persons, it would do well for some basic education getting out to the whole faith community about how to respond to grief. This could be an event, a weekly Lenten devotional, or even shared in monthly printed communication. The grief and mourning of bereaved persons from the congregation could be brought significant comfort by some simple understandings about what to do and what to say, so as to not leave them feeling isolated or like a pariah in the community. (Appendix 2 includes lists of helpful and not-so-helpful things to say and do to be more sensitive to someone who is bereaved.)

While one would not want to make a person feel as if the whole congregation was talking about them and their grief behind their backs, an encouragement to the congregational members to engage in a very simple and sensitive contact should be a natural part of the education of the community. This might avoid the church version of what I call, "The Great Supermarket Dodge." This occurs in a grocery store when a newly bereaved person is pushing their cart down the aisle. At the other end of the aisle, someone they know and who, in previous times, would have come up to them and chatted, sees them, and abruptly turns their cart to go another way rather than risking coming into contact with another's grief. The faith community version of this might be at the greeting time during the worship service or at coffee hour. Anytime someone is avoided by people who would have previously made a friendly approach, it is a "dodge" and the grieving person knows it and feels it. Every time this example has been shared in grief groups or workshops; participants all say that they can relate to the avoidance that is a part of the dodge.

It is not like everyone in the community needs to have a script or become a grief counselor. It may be enough to simply know that it is not intrusive to walk up to someone and share a moment. It may be best to avoid asking, "How are you?" That just leaves the griever trying to come up with the answer for which they think that the other person is looking. Much better to say, "I've been thinking about you" while placing a hand on their shoulder or just shaking their hand. If they want to talk about where they are in their grief journey, they will. Even better, sit down next to them, look them in the eye and say nothing. Absolutely nothing. Some of the best grief work is done in complete silence. It has been noted that, in the biblical story of Job, his three friends came to console him in his heart-rending grief. They sat by his side silently, without saying a word. They were just there. Seven days and seven nights they remained silent at his side. After that, they started to talk … and ruined everything.

The faith community bears a profound responsibility to those in its midst who are grieving. No one should have to grieve alone, and no one should be expected to meet someone else's expectations of how the grief journey should be undertaken. One of the phrases that is used to indicate church membership is that someone "belongs" to such-and-such church or synagogue. To belong is more than just membership. It should mean that everyone can be in the faith community when they are celebrating life changes or grieving life changes. The faith community may be the only group of persons in their lives who can hear the heart-rending grief and stand by while tears flow freely, listening to the stories told over and over because it is how a griever tries to make sense of what has happened and what has been lost.

The casseroles are long gone, and dishes have been returned. Everyone is ready to get back to the tasks at hand and move forward. Yet there is a widow who stares across the dinner table at the empty place occupied by her husband of fifty years, and she wonders if anyone else will listen to her stories. A husband and wife stand at the door of their deceased child's bedroom and wonder what to do with her things, with his sports trophies, with the stuffed animals that once brought such comfort. Who will hold them as they weep?

Where will they turn? Who will listen? Who will be there to offer a gentle touch, a simple word of caring, or a shared tear? If not their community of faith, then who?

CHAPTER 4 — A NEW RECIPE

Rob and Janie were semi-regular attendees of worship services in a small Protestant Christian congregation in a rural community. They lived in the country with their horses and a few cows but were mostly retired from ranching. When the pastor and his family accepted their invitation to supper one evening, they were told by the couple that they were supportive of the ministry being provided and enjoyed being in church when they could. What they most wanted to convey, however, was why they would never place membership in that or any other congregation. Years before, when their young adult son was tragically killed in an accident, the church they were attending at the time did all the right "casserole" things in the days around the death and funeral. After that, after the casseroles were gone, they felt the church left them on their own to deal with everything that went with this tragic loss and the grief that had wrapped the family. Rob said, "I won't join another church and I won't give to the church on a regular basis. But if you, as a pastor, ever have a special project that you need some funds to get done, come and see me, and I'll help where I can." The old cowboy was still hurting from his loss and what he saw as the failure of his church years before. But he was also true to his word and was approached by the pastor on more than one occasion to help with special programs or projects and he always came through. Yet he never forgave the church as a whole for its tragic failure.

Casseroles are helpful whether tasty or not. They open doors to help interact with grievers, and they fill not just stomachs, but they also fill hearts with gratitude in a difficult time. Casseroles are important. After they are gone, however, the question that needs to be asked is: Now what? When the world is done with its initial response to bereaved persons, what will come next? What is the nature of the grief that persons and families are experiencing in the aftermath of a death? What can help and how do we get there?

Not everyone who experiences a significant loss will need formal grief therapy. About 80% of bereaved persons will be able to manage their grief as that grief comes to journey with them. The other 20% will find themselves struggling with grief that is complicated by any number of factors and will find themselves with a Gordian Knot that may need a trained grief therapist to unravel. Some of the 80% might respond to a grief support group of one kind or another. There they can gain insight into their bereavement process and discover that others are experiencing many of the same feelings and emotions, a realization which, in itself, can be very helpful and affirming.

Many faith communities will not have someone trained and comfortable leading a bereavement group, even if there are enough people to form a group. Therefore, faith community leaders need to have community referrals available for those who experience traumatic, complicated, or chronic grief and referrals to active grief support programs that offer the group experience for those looking to connect on that level.

The vast majority of people who grieve do not necessarily reach out nor do they raise any flags that would indicate that they need anything from the faith community in response to their grief. What that means is that if people find support for their grief, the faith community can be a supportive family of persons who can reach out with understanding and caring, especially at significant times of the bereaved person's journey with grief. It is also true that many will only struggle with some grief-related issues later on, after it appeared or was reported that they needed little to no support.

The process (not "program") suggested here is designed to follow the bereaved person through at least the first year after their loss. It is an effort to stay invested in their life and grief process on a level that is both helpful and non-intrusive. Such follow-up and available support would necessitate some education of leaders and some members of the faith community in areas of grief and bereavement. The reasoning behind a somewhat formal or designed process comes from realities concerning how groups in general and faith communities in particular function and out of this author's experience.

While clergy or faith community leaders are actively involved as participants and leaders of the process, it is important that much of the contact comes from laypersons. Grief support including bereavement visits or contact is seen as something that would normally be expected from their clergy persons. It is important that the bereaved see this process as a caring and very intentional act of the faith community above and beyond what one might normally expect.

It is this author's experience that any program or process that is instituted needs to have active buy-in by members of the congregation and leadership from laypersons as well as clergy. Activities that initially begin with lots of enthusiasm, but no lay leadership and ownership can predictably begin to fade away over a short amount of time, leaving the clergy to pick up the slack or just watch it die.

It is important that there be a team of people trained for this process. Not everyone is like the Apostle Paul who became "all things to all people." Some people just don't always emotionally or culturally fit together as helpfully as we would hope. There may be personality differences or differences in life experience, culture, etc. that make it difficult for one particular caregiver to connect on a helpful level with the bereaved person. Therefore, it is suggested that there be multiple people involved so that the most helpful match can be made, or a match changed as necessary.

People all grieve in different ways and according to different timetables, but there are fairly predictable time spans and events that suggest when contact might be most beneficial. And, of course, one of the reasons for such a thoughtfully planned response to grief will allow someone in the congregation to note things going on with the bereaved parishioner that might call for further or more frequent contact. Regular contacts and updates by lay volunteers with the faith community leader are crucial throughout the process of follow-up and visitation.

Another good reason for such a detailed process of bereavement follow-up is the importance of accountability. If such a process is announced and launched within the faith community, consistency and transparency will be key. Having a process with set or suggested timelines and responsibilities will give people the sense that, not only is the faith community reaching out and caring for bereaved persons they know, but it also provides the promise that the faith community will be there in the same way for them and their families when similar ministry is needed.

Following a set or detailed process is important because, when it comes to grief, as with so many things in life, timing is everything. At the risk of contradicting the above statements about the nature and uniqueness of grief, there are some fairly typical markers along the grief journey that would be opportune times to check in with persons who have suffered a loss. Some of those will even come well after the one-year anniversary of the death. This process will provide opportunities for checking in at certain typical or even more unique times in the life of those who have suffered a loss. Examples include wedding anniversaries, special holiday times, as well as relatively normal markers that would have been celebratory points in the life of a deceased child or adolescent (i.e., the age for getting a driver's license, graduating from high school, etc.).

The terms around this topic of what is experienced after a death are often confused or mistakenly used interchangeably. "Bereavement" refers to a state in which something cherished has been lost; being without something dear to you. You can be bereft of almost anything important to you. When something dear or vital to you has been taken away, whether it be a person or a prized possession, you are bereaved in that you are deprived of that object or person. "Grief" consists of the internal thoughts and feelings you have after experiencing a loss. This encompasses the emotional, physical, spiritual, and behavioral outcomes of a loss. "Mourning" is the process one goes through in grief or giving expression to your grief. A person or group's mourning may be a factor of culture or familial customs as to how grief is expressed or addressed. While all cultures experience grief and have ways of mourning loss, they can appear quite different from one another. You do not have to travel the world to see these cultural differences. Even among North American and other distinctively Western populations, the ways that people mourn and the funeral practices that are typical for a geographic region can vary quite a bit. One only has to picture the mourning process carried out for a political dignitary versus an old-fashioned New Orleans jazz funeral to see just how divergent mourning and funeral trends can be.

One important step in providing assistance and ministry to persons after they have experienced a loss is to help them normalize their internal and external feelings. Grief and mourning are not signs of weakness and are not a sign of mental illness. "Grief is neither a disorder nor a healing process; it is a sign of health itself, a whole and natural gesture of love."[9]

Yet, as universal as grief is, it is also unique and individual in its nature and expression. There is no right or wrong way to grieve or mourn. It is important that people who are responding or reaching out to those who grieve know to refrain from trying to compare that person's grief with their own grief. Your way of experiencing grief, however helpful it might have been for you, may not be helpful at all to someone else.

There are many emotions that will be encountered, especially in times near the death. There may be anger at the person who died or anger at a system that is believed to have hastened or contributed to their death. Emotions might include feelings of guilt for commissions or omissions of which the bereaved may feel they

---

9   Charles A. Corr, Clyde M. Nabe, and Donna M. Corr, *Death and Dying: Life and Living,* 4th edition, (Belmont, CA: Wadsworth/Thomson Learning), p. 214.

were a part, a sense of relief for the deceased or for themselves, a sense of helplessness at not being able to prevent a death, or fear for other loved ones still living. All these feelings and many more may be in evidence as one listens to a person talk about their grief. It is important to listen to and accept their feelings without discounting those feelings and expressions of grief. To say, "you shouldn't feel guilty" or "you shouldn't be angry" merely closes the conversation and creates a situation where the bereaved may end up swallowing their grief and not sharing for fear of similar admonitions for them to not feel what they are feeling.

Several factors can contribute to an individual's grief process; contribute, not determine. The list of factors includes the age of the deceased and the griever, gender, the griever's relationship with the deceased, the circumstances of the death (i.e., elderly and sick versus young and traumatic), the support system available to the bereaved, cultural and/or spiritual background, and their own grieving styles that they have experienced previously. For instance, grieving the death of my elderly and ill parents was different than grieving the unexpected death of my sister. In each case, I had grief but my relationship with each family member, the manner of their death and what led up to it, to say nothing of my experience as a hospital chaplain and many other things, helped to shape and color the grief that I felt, and still feel, for each.

While the process described here is designed to follow along the first year after a death, it does not suggest that there is any time when grief ends. An unfortunate term that came into the culture of grief is "closure." Funeral rites are sometimes thought to be necessary to "bring closure" for the grief-stricken people. I believe that viewing a body after a death is important for most all persons when possible. The viewing does not "create closure", as some suggest. The term "closure" might leave the bereaved believing that because something should bring closure, it might mark an endpoint or goal to their grief and wondering why their grief is not "closed".

There is not necessarily any end to grief. The way we experience grief generally changes through time and life experiences. As one would imagine, to never move beyond the terrible, soul-ripping feelings experienced immediately after a tragic loss would not be healthy or helpful. This complicated mourning or chronic grief would best be referred to a professional who is trained to work with individuals who experience grief reactions that severely hamper normal life experience and functioning.

This type of grief is fairly rare and can respond well to appropriate counseling. Most of us, however, will experience grief that comes to live and journey with us after the loss of someone dear and will continue to share our journey on some level as long as we live. The grief will change over time and circumstances, but it never really leaves us. Whenever we are reminded of a particular memory that is truly representative of that person or our relationship with them, there is sometimes a noted "twang" of the heartstrings that reminds us that we still miss that person and always will. That does not mean we will fold up with tearful, heart-rending grief each time. It's only that the memory itself says that they are not absent from our mind or experience, and we are sorry they are gone. When people ask me how they will know they are getting over their grief, I assure them that they will not get over it. However, someday when memories come up, they will find themselves smiling more than crying, chuckling instead of weeping. When that begins to occur, they will know that the journey with grief is becoming manageable. As our grief journeys with us, it will, over time, take more of a back seat in our daily experience but there still is not a finish line for the grief journey as long as the memory stays alive.

There have been several attempts to give some kind of order to the grief process by seeing it in certain stages that one must go through or traverse on their way to some relief from the grief experience. When I was a young man going through college in the mid-1970s, the truly groundbreaking work of Elizabeth Kubler-Ross was the standard for describing grief.[10] Her five stages beginning with denial and isolation and ending with acceptance were never intended to be a description of grief following a death.

10 Elizabeth Kubler-Ross, *On Death and Dying*, (New York, NY, The MacMillan Co., 1969).

Her research and insights were based on her work with terminally ill patients in the hospital setting as they went from first hearing the difficult news that they were dying to a possible point of acceptance of their imminent death. It was never intended to be a description of specific stages of grief that a person must encounter or endure to get through grief following the death of someone close.

There have been several stage-type theories or descriptions of phases of grief put forward. The most helpful (in my opinion) and most widely accepted method of setting out some roadmap of the journey of grief is the four tasks of mourning as set forth by William Worden. While they are not steps or stages that must be completed in a particular order, Worden states that all four tasks must be completed before mourning can be completed. Note that he never suggests that grief can be completed but that mourning, which he defines as "the adaptation to loss" needs to complete the tasks. Those tasks are: 1) to accept the reality of the loss; 2) to work through the pain of grief; 3) to adjust to the environment in which the deceased is missing; 4) to emotionally relocate the deceased and move on with life.[11]

Dr. Kenneth Doka later suggested a fifth task to round out Worden's original four. That fifth task has to do with reviewing faith and meaning. Sometimes a loss can present a challenge to our spirituality, our faith practice or our assumptions. This fifth task would be "to rebuild faith and philosophical systems that are challenged by loss." After a loss, we sometimes need to review how it is that our faith or spirituality speaks to us or informs our life. Dr. Doka suggests that a part of this review of faith or spirituality might include a question about what resources a person has available to them after a loss and that would include our beliefs, rituals, and, significantly for this book and process, what community resources do we have?[12]

---

11 William Worden, *Grief Counseling and Grief Therapy,* 3rd edition, (New York, NY: Springer Publishing Co, 1991. There is now a 5th edition of Worden's work, which is a testament to the helpfulness and veracity of his theory and practice.

12 Kenneth Doka, "The Spiritual Crisis of Bereavement," *Death and Spirituality*, Kenneth Doka, ed., (Amityville, NY: Baywood Publishing, 1993), pp. 190-191.

For all this talk about how grief and mourning progress, the reality is that grief is there because we loved or were attached to something or someone that is now gone. How we get through that is very individual. Grief is never neat and tidy. Regardless of what we need to do to ameliorate grief on some level, there are many ways to get there. One attendant of a grief group simply described her grief as "3 steps forward and 2 steps back." Another talked of grief coming and going like waves, and still another talked of grief being a spiral. Some people will step into their grief knowing that the only way through is to go through. Others will be more tentative and demonstrate an approach/avoidance kind of dance with their grief. One of the first things I have learned to request from someone who asks for assistance with their grief is: "Teach me about your grief." They are the only expert and the only first-person witness to their grief process that no other can prescribe or accurately predict.

The very best support that can be provided to those who grieve is compassionate understanding, an occasional shoulder to wet with tears, and a patient, listening ear. There is no magic to it. There is no fixing grief and there is no expiration date on our mourning. With some of the exceptions already noted, grief will go through whatever rocky, hilly, and confusing path it chooses. Nothing can change that, but appropriate caring shared by appropriately trained individuals who can become waystations along the road can make the journey with grief a little less daunting. Such a ministry may give hope and comfort to make the journey less lonely and help the bereaved find their way. Who better to be the guides and porters for such a journey than trained and available members of a person's faith community, who are ready to journey alongside, and sometimes shoulder some of the burden that can make this journey seem so overwhelming?

CHAPTER 5 — COOKING IT UP

Word comes that there has been a death in the family of a member of the faith community. The pastor or spiritual leader makes immediate contact with the next-of-kin and visits to provide caring ministry and set a time to meet to make arrangements for a service.

At the same time, the congregation's phone tree shifts into high gear. Those nearest to the next of kin may call the family right away or even stop by the home to offer sincere condolences. Some may bring food and/or try to ascertain what the basic and physical needs of the family will be during the next few days.

Food arrives, offers of assistance with transportation or child-care are given, and funeral or memorial service plans are finalized. The service happens on whatever level chosen by the family followed by the obligatory reception which may involve a luncheon, finger foods, or just coffee and cookies.

When the casseroles are gone, and nothing but crumbs remain on the cookie platters, people around the bereaved family begin to move on with their lives, which may or may not have been directly impacted by the death. The family members begin to slowly come out of the fog, which is a God-given defense mechanism, allowing those who are bereaved to ease into the reality of life without their loved one. The family's slow (sometimes very slow) return to reality is normal and will occur in its own time. Also normal is the need of those not as close to the deceased or family to move back into life at their usual pace. Both are normal and natural ways of dealing with death. Someone recently bereaved cannot quickly shift gears and move back into the former rhythms of life as it was before the death. People not directly involved in the life of the deceased or family cannot suspend their lives indefinitely but will move back into life soon after the services have been completed. People who were there to offer support at the time of death and the days following will move on leaving the bereaved to find their way back into the new normal that is now their life. The question is, who or what will step into that gap to provide informed and compassionate support to the bereaved through the days, weeks, and months to come?

Such is the very ministry that a trained and committed cadre of persons who, with appropriate leadership and a designed process, would be ready to provide. From the first notification of the death, a standard but flexible process would be set in motion that would assure the bereaved that they will not have to go through their grief in isolation or without the direct ministry of their faith community.

The involvement of the bereaved is, of course, optional. There will always be people who do not want to talk about their grief with others or do not wish to be singled out for special ministry. They can decline to be included in the process or they can pick and choose the parts or portions of the ministry in which they might want to be involved. What is important is that the ministry is offered and that they know their faith community recognizes their loss and is prepared and willing to meet them where they are and walk with them through part of their journey with grief.

THE PERSONS SELECTED FOR THE BEREAVEMENT TEAM

Choosing the appropriate people for such a ministry is not always easy. In some cases, the faith community might already have a functioning lay visitation team of some sort. This might be a Stephen Ministry team that involves members who receive significant training in caring for others. There may be a group of people who have committed to and have been trained to make visits and maybe offer sacraments in homes, skilled nursing facilities, and hospitals. Persons from such pre-existing ministries might choose to also be a part of a Bereavement Team, having already had some training and some experience in member visitation. It is vital, however, that the team be selected with the specific goal of grief support in mind.

When considering the persons in the faith community who would be ideal for providing the contact involved with this process, it would be best to avoid persons who are professional counselors, doctors, or others highly trained in people-helping skills. Again, this is not a counseling program but a designed process for responding to those who are grieving. That is not to say that such professionals would not be excellent resources to provide some training and equipping for the persons who are directly involved.

It would be beneficial if team members had some direct experience with death and grief. That does not necessarily require people who have had a close, direct experience with particular types of losses (i.e., spousal loss, death of a child, sibling loss, etc.). While it might be helpful to match team members with those who have suffered a similar loss, that is not necessary. It is difficult, however, to relate to those who grieve if one has personally never faced their own grief on some level.

On the other hand, it would be a mistake to choose someone for the team who is freshly bereaved. A good but general rule of thumb would be that those who volunteer to assist in such a ministry be at least one year out from their own loss. This is the rule for some, if not most, hospice organizations accepting new volunteers to work with dying patients and their families. Otherwise, the experiences of the person with whom they are working could easily trigger emotions and memories that might get in the way of their ability to listen and respond appropriately. It is okay to shed tears in the presence of a grieving person's tears or sadness. When the caregiver's own suffering matches or overshadows that of the griever, however, it is time to step aside, allowing another team member to follow that particular bereaved person.

Related to that, it would be appropriate that persons on the team be individuals who have a healthy and open attitude toward death and dying. Such work is not for everyone. People who tend to feel helpless in the face of someone's overwhelming sadness or possibly open demonstrations of grief would not do well as direct care members of the team. This includes the ability to be comfortable and patient in silence. Sometimes a silent presence says more than all the advice offered verbally.

An open attitude towards dying and grief would also necessitate a nonjudgmental presence and approach that brings comfort and a willingness to listen, not to judge or fix anyone else's grief. We bring the gift of presence, of just being there to listen and to bear witness to the sometimes-raw pain of grief without trying to take it away or explain it with the best-intentioned platitudes. Again, to quote Megan Divine: "Unacknowledged and unheard pain doesn't go away. One of the reasons our culture is so messed up around grief is that we've tried to erase pain before it's had its say. We've got an emotional backlog sitting in our hearts."[13]

It might go without saying but we will say it anyway; anyone who wishes to be a part of a faith community bereavement team needs to have excellent communication skills. Yes, silence is important, but the time comes to communicate verbally. When faced with overwhelming things, we humans tend to jump in with whatever we got, no matter how correct, helpful, or unhelpful it might be. Team members must avoid the temptation to say things of which they do not have a full understanding. In other words, "stay in your lane."

The other essential issue with communication is that confidentiality is crucial. While it is likely true that other members of the faith community know about the death, maybe the circumstances of the death and even how the bereaved is feeling about the death, what is discussed and experienced in the role of a bereavement team member is not something for sharing with other church members.

---

13   Devine, *It's Ok That You're Not OK*, p. 87.

We all know how easily and quickly a helpful relationship can be derailed when one hears that their confidence has been broken.

What training is given will not encompass everything that a bereaved person needs to know or hear. It is important to know one's own competency. If something comes up that is out of the wheelhouse of the team member, they can let the bereaved know that while this is not something they know enough about, they will take the concern or question back to the faith community leader who will find or offer the needed information. This can also avoid the temptation to move beyond our task as listeners and caregivers by trying to offer actual counseling about grief or other life topics.

Finally, on a more theological note, the team members should not feel it necessary to defend God, their faith, or the faith community, when bereaved persons ask questions about the role of God in the death or the grief journey. Such discussions as well as discussions of the afterlife should be left up to the clergy/leader of the faith community.

THE ACTUAL RECIPE

The two main components of this process involve direct phone calls, hopefully leading to home visits, as well as a mailing program. What is laid out below is a suggested timeline for a response, but not something that is proven through research at this point. It is designed to be set in motion starting from the date of the funeral or memorial service. In situations where the memorial service is delayed until weeks or even months after the death, however, one would not want to wait for the service to occur before activating the Bereavement Team but instead do so within a couple of weeks after the death.

After the team member best suited for a particular bereaved family is chosen by the faith community leader or the Bereavement Team leader and has accepted the responsibility, there should be a meeting with the faith community leader or team leader. The team member can be filled in a bit about the family, the death, and any special circumstances that might be important. All of this is to be done, of course, without breaking confidence. If there is information that is truly private, the family will tell their visitor if they want them to know.

The following is a suggestion for the timing of visits and mailings. More complete suggested process forms are located in Appendix 1.

VISITATION

2 Weeks—team member visit

6 Weeks—clergy or faith community leader visit

12 Weeks—team member visit (if bereaved has not been back to services or activities, offer to pick them up and be with them)

24 Weeks—clergy visit and assessment

36 Weeks—team member calls to assess ongoing visitation needs—visit if bereaved wishes a visit

52 Weeks—clergy visit, and assessment is made for possible ongoing support

This is just an outline of the bare minimum number of contacts. Some bereaved people or families may wish for additional contact, or their situation might suggest the need of greater frequency of contact. For instance, an elderly person who has lost a spouse and whose family does not live nearby may relish the idea of a weekly phone call and frequent visits by someone so they have a person with whom to share, as well as someone who might be able to help with some of the many tasks that are left to be completed after a death. There is so much to deal with in the wake of a death. There is paperwork, decisions about what to do with the clothing and personal possessions of the deceased, and thank you cards to write and mail, among many other things. Under the best of circumstances, grief leaves one in a bit of a fog and it often impacts memory. If there is no close family, the Bereavement Team might be of tremendous support as the bereaved try to navigate all the confusing oceans of tasks with which they have been left.

BEREAVEMENT MAILINGS

The timing suggested below matches up with the suggested visit schedule above to create a sense of continuity so that there is some contact from the faith community within reasonable windows of time. If the timing seems complex, some might find it easier to just send out a mailing monthly or every other month.

Week 1 – Condolence card signed by clergy and Bereavement Team

Week 6 –

Week 10 –

Week 18 –

Week 32 –

Week 48 –

Week 52 –

These mailings, other than the initial condolence mailing, do not have to be something distinctly personal or even written by someone in the faith community. Many resources provide options for a bereavement mailing program. Some provide information for a small cost that can be used (such as Centering Grief Resources, Resources for Grief, and the "Journey's" mailing from the Hospice Foundation of America). One could also go to the website of some hospice organizations to find things that they would readily share. Let's not forget the resources often available from your local funeral homes and cemeteries in print or on their websites. It is important, however, to have anything included in mailings reviewed by someone who understands grief and loss so that the faith community is not seen as sending out information that is more hurtful than helpful. There are plenty of both to be found out there.

The material within the mailings does not always need to be necessarily informative, although some of it will likely discuss the grief process. It can include poetry, stories, scripture verse, photography, or anything else that would have a positive impact on those going along the journey with grief. It would be good to have some specific items that might have a special impact on the bereaved that could be included in mailings around holidays.[14]

Once the program is set up with which mailings are to go out at specific intervals, then the same mailings can be used for other families as other deaths occur. Keeping track of when mailings go out to a given family can be confusing. It is suggested that there be one person whose primary responsibility is keeping track of the mailing process. There might be a person interested in the bereavement ministry but who is not comfortable making home visits or physically able to do so. Such a valued person or persons could do all of the mailings and possibly keep tabs on the calls or visits made by visiting team members.

The process described here is by no means a rigid system that will fit every faith community or circumstance. It is merely an attempt to put some organization to a ministry opportunity that might bring true blessings to persons who have experienced a death and to members of a Bereavement Team as well.

There are certainly many things that such a team could take on as ministry projects in addition to the visitation. Creating a memorial garden on the property of the faith community, for instance, or planting a special tree on the property with a plaque dedicating the tree in memory of members who have died. Raising funds for, and designing, a memorial wall with names of deceased members. Someone might write a small memorial article about the deceased, as described by the family, including the deceased's contribution to the faith community, that could be printed in the church newsletter. The possibilities are endless. Anything that serves the needs of those who grieve can be a part of this ministry.

Holidays, especially Christmas, can be exceedingly difficult in the first and second years after a death. Team members could offer to ease some of the sadness or burden by proposing to go Christ-

---

14 Appendix 3 includes some sample materials that could be used for the
    mailings.

mas shopping with the bereaved or do their shopping for them. It may be difficult to bring oneself to decorate their Christmas tree or house, or wrap presents but if those things are wanted and important, team members could pitch in to help out with many such tasks.

This Bereavement Team process is much more than a simple home visitation program to widows and widowers. It is a rich ministry that can open up opportunities for real healing to take place in the lives of those who are grieving. It also opens the door for an entire faith community to understand the nature of grief, the importance of recognizing and honoring a person's grief, and the community's responsibility to walk along with people as they journey with their grief.

Kenneth Mitchell and Herbert Anderson, in their writing on pastoral care and grief, speak to a community's need to be with those who grieve. "Although grieving is by its very nature a lonely task, the resolution of grief requires the presence of other persons.... Full release from the hold that emotions of any kind have on us depends on their being heard. Grieving is in part an interpersonal process, lonely though it may be."[15]

Everyone who loves will grieve. Everyone who grieves needs to be loved and heard.

---

15 Kenneth Mitchell and Herbert Anderson, *All Our Losses All Our Griefs: Resources for Pastoral Care,* (Louisville, KY: Westminster John Knox Press, 1983), p. 107.

CHAPTER 6 — SERVING IT UP

After the casseroles are gone and once the tables in the Fellowship Hall have been wiped clean by those saints who always remain behind to clean up, more nourishment in the form of grief support is being prepared to be served. Now, however, the soul-healing nutrition will come to the bereaved members of the faith community and be served to them right where they are physically, emotionally, and spiritually. The recipe outlined in chapter 5 is now ready to be served. Those who will be serving it up must understand the nature of grief and what they might encounter as they provide grief support.

By way of analogy, before opening their doors for dining each evening, fine restaurants gather the serving staff to show them the menu for the evening and allow them to taste new items on the menu. This way they are prepared to offer and describe the menu for the customer. It is not just basic descriptions on a stained ten-year-old menu but specific information about flavor, spiciness, and types of preparation from someone who has tasted it. If the servers know their stuff, they might even know which wine to recommend that would best pair with your entrée.

When it comes to the topic of bereavement, grief, and mourning, most everyone knows what it is and recognizes it as the loss of something to which one is attached and the feelings and expression of loss. Over the past forty to fifty years researchers and clinicians have added tremendously to our understanding of the grief process and what it entails. Before that, the research was minimal. Early in

the 20th Century, Sigmund Freud wrote about the loss of attachment and the necessity of completing one's "grief work" in order
to cope. Later John Bowlby would expand on "attachment theory"
and the struggle to cling to or recover that which has been lost. In
1944, Eric Linderman produced a seminal work that expanded on
the nature of grief work that all bereaved persons must experience.[16]

In modern times the one-size-fits-all types of grief theories
have been challenged and expanded upon by the understanding
that grief is unique to each individual and is influenced by many
different situational factors.

Understanding Styles of Grief and Mourning

When referring to styles of mourning, two of the primary
styles that are often spoken about have been the traditional male
and female styles of mourning. It was thought that the female style
of mourning was more demonstrative and open while the male style
was much more stoic and internal. The research and writing of Kenneth Doka and Terry Martin opened a whole new understanding
of styles of mourning as it relates to gender. Research and practice
demonstrated that assigning certain styles of mourning based on
gender was to fail to understand and appreciate the breadth of
emotions and styles that are well beyond gender designations. The
terms that Kenneth Doka and Terry Martin came to use to describe
a continuum of mourning styles are "intuitive" and "instrumental"
grieving and mourning.[17]

Those on the intuitive side of the grieving spectrum are more
likely to be openly expressive of their inner feelings. They are generally comforted by talking about their experience of grief with
others and are open to exploration of their grief. Intuitive grievers
find comfort in the ability to share their feelings, respond to active

16   DeSpelder and Strickland. *The Last Dance,* pp. 281-283.
17   Kenneth Doka and Terry Martin, *Grieving Beyond Gender: Understanding
     the Ways Men and Women Grieve,* revised edition, (New York, NY,
     Routledge, 2010).

listening, and may exhibit low physical energy. The loss they feel on the inside is openly mourned on the outside.

Those on the instrumental side of the grieving spectrum are likely to find their expression of grief coming through cognitive or physical/behavioral activities. Feelings tend to be less intense than for intuitive grievers and they may be reluctant to talk about their inner feelings of grief.

One might say that intuitive grievers need to share their grief. Instrumental grievers are more likely to try to understand their feelings in an effort to regain some sense of control and work out their feelings in a physical or technical manner.

Like so much else in the area of grief, there is no right or wrong. One must see this not as an either/or situation but rather a continuum, with nearly no one exhibiting extremes on either the intuitive or instrumental ends of the continuum. There are no female or male styles of grief. Females tend to be on the intuitive side with males often leaning toward the instrumental side of the continuum. Some males grieve in a more intuitive manner and there are females who are very instrumental in their grieving style.

Failure to understand these differences and how they play out in the lives of grievers can sometimes be problematic when it is assumed that a person should grieve in a manner not consistent with their natural style. Back in the day, I can remember being told that if a person did not openly mourn, they were not doing grief properly. Everyone had to have tears for grief to be complete. This can sometimes create problems around a death when the family struggles to understand, honor, and support one another's natural grieving styles.

When a toddler died in a tragic accident, the parents struggled with this very issue. The mother, who was strongly intuitive, was open with her grief and had close friends with whom she shared feelings and tears. She could not understand why her husband was not grieving in the same manner and it was causing a rift in their relationship. The husband, who leaned far over on the instrumental side of the spectrum, was out in his shop quietly building a casket for his little girl. Both were grieving in the only way they knew how. What was needed was for each to understand their unique but normal grieving styles and to find ways to support their partner's manner of mourning. Grieving or mourning were not lacking. What was lacking was an understanding of their different styles of grieving and an openness to support each other in the reality of how their individual grief and mourning got expressed. I fully cringe when I look back on my early ministry and the times, I commented that, when people were not openly mourning, their ability to deal with grief would be compromised.

THE DUAL PROCESS MODEL

As emotional as mourning can be and as life-consuming as grief can be, one cannot live within the bounds of grief all of the time. While early on in a significant grief process, one might feel they are drowning in grief, it is necessary and natural to occasionally come up for air.

As a result of their groundbreaking research, Margaret Stroebe and Henk Schut presented a model for understanding how people cope with grief. They recognized that the idea of a relentless grief process without periods of diversion or time off from the emotional and cognitive work of grieving was neither realistic nor healthy. Persons may choose to take some time away from their grief or choose distraction of mind and emotion for a time. The Dual Process Model suggests that most people who grieve will, from time to time, oscillate between a "Loss Orientation" and a "Restoration Orientation" as they move through their lives post-loss. Below is the model as designed by Stroebe and Schut that is now accepted as a reasonable picture of normal grief coping for most individuals.

Loss-Oriented coping includes such things as physical sensations of grief, feelings of anger, frustration, loneliness, unfinished business, coping with special days, dealing with the possessions of the deceased, and coping with the pressures from other well-meaning people.

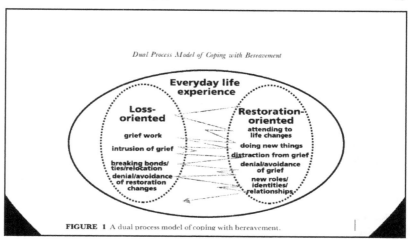

FIGURE 1 A dual process model of coping with bereavement.

Restoration-oriented coping would involve the griever in such things as, goal setting, taking a break from grief, meeting one's own health needs, learning new skills, re-connecting with friends, establishing new friendships, experiencing new forms of entertainment, setting realistic expectations, and volunteering or working. Over time healthy coping will involve an ongoing oscillation between the two coping styles. This is how normal grief progresses, moving between an orientation that focuses on the loss and an orientation that focuses on the restoration of life and function.

Understanding this model can be very helpful when someone tells a team member, for instance, that they laughed for the first time since the death and feel terribly guilty for laughing. Some people feel that it is disrespectful to go out and have some fun or do new things that bring pleasure. At such times, the griever can be assured that they can expect to go through this oscillation throughout the grieving process and that it is both a natural and a healthy way of coping with their loss.[18]

---

18 Margaret Stroebe and Henk Schut, "The Dual Model of Coping with Bereavement: Rationale and Description," *Death Studies* (23:3, 1999): p. 197-224.

DISENFRANCHISED GRIEF

Disenfranchised grief is a term that refers to a loss that is unrecognized or which cannot be disclosed for any number of reasons. Such disenfranchisement can cause a person who has experienced a loss to hide or minimize their grief, thereby preventing them from receiving the needed support that would normally be offered to a griever.

In some cases, disenfranchised grief results from the fact that the relationship is not recognized as one that would warrant grief. There are many relationships that may not be seen as necessarily close, but which might bring significant grief when a death occurs. Such losses might include ex-spouses, colleagues, illicit lovers, in-laws, friends, or pets. Any loss that involves a relationship that convention says should not be close enough to cause grief reactions or relationships that cannot be revealed lead to disenfranchisement leaving persons stuck with a grief that is unrecognized and unsupported. There are times when even very close faith communities can enter into a communal silence, not acknowledging a death and resulting grief, when relationships are not sanctioned or recognized by the social or faith stance of the members.

Grief can also be disenfranchised when the loss itself is not recognized. This might involve such things as miscarriages, abortion, or foster parents. Under the category of miscarriages, while in some cases the woman will receive support for the loss, often it is her spouse or partner whose grief seems out of place to others.

A third category of disenfranchisement comes about when the griever as a person is not recognized. Under this category are people who are mentally disabled, very old, or seen as too young to be able to experience true grief.

In all of these ways, grievers can be bereft of not only a person of significance they have lost but also bereft of the support they may desperately need. "Disenfranchisement can occur when a society inhibits grief by establishing 'grieving norms' that deny grief to persons deemed to have insignificant losses, insignificant relationships, or an insignificant capacity to grieve."[19]

Phrases that reveal a lack of appropriate support, leaving a griever and their grief or loss disenfranchised include such things as: "after all, he was very old," "at least you didn't have a chance to get to know your baby and you can always get pregnant again," "she's too young to understand what's going on," "you've been divorced for ten years," or "they are in a better place." Anything that belittles or negates the grief that is felt leaves people alone in their grief, unable to talk about the loss or their feelings. A significant loss is always a loss, and grief is always grief, regardless of what social convention, religious beliefs, or community norms might have to say about it.

There was a wonderful woman in one of the congregations I served who was a model of Christian faith. There was a period of something like twelve or fifteen years that she diligently and lovingly cared for her blind and disabled husband. A few weeks after his death she came to my office with a surprising statement. She believed she had lost her faith. When I asked what brought her to that conclusion, she said that if she had a strong Christian faith, she should be happy that her husband was in heaven and no longer suffering from the pain and indignities that had marked so much of the last part of his life. But instead of being happy for him, she felt sad and was grieving the loss of her husband of some sixty years. It was hard for her to justify her legitimate grief with the faith she felt should negate her sense of sadness and grief. In essence, this wonderful woman was disenfranchising her own grief and causing herself tremendous but unnecessary turmoil of faith, mind, and heart.

SECONDARY LOSSES

Whenever a person experiences a loss, whether through death, divorce, moving, or other circumstances, the primary loss is the

19 Doka, Kenneth, ed., *Disenfranchised Grief: New Directions, Challenges and Strategies for Practice,* (Champaign, IL: Research Press, 2002), p. xiii.

person or the relationship. With nearly every loss, however, especially loss through death, there are bound to be secondary losses. These secondary losses come about as a result of the primary loss and must also be faced and grieved over time.

If parents lose a child, one of their secondary losses might be who they have been up to the time of the death. When Sally was alive, they had roles like mother, father, parents, Sally's parents, the PTA president, the classroom volunteer, and the parent whose yard where all the neighborhood kids used to congregate. Along with the loss of roles comes the loss of relationships. In this case, relationships with Sally's friends, the parents of the friends, and others who were in the lives of the parents were only because they were Sally's family.

When parents die, sometimes the family cohesion goes away, or long-treasured traditions fade away. When my parents and parents-in-law died, I was no longer anyone's child or son. I was no longer a son-in-law. The unique things that I shared with that older generation were gone and they were sometimes things I had to mourn. I had to grieve the fact that I did not have someone who understood cars, electricity, or DIY projects, whom I could call for advice because both of the men who knew all those things were gone.

At times, a death can leave us with many roles that had become a normal and important part of our life. The role of caregiver for an aging or ill family member, for instance, can be all-consuming, therefore creating a gaping hole in one's life and experience after the death. If the breadwinner in the family dies, a spouse might lose the role of stay-at-home parent so they can get a full-time job. One might lose their home or other securities in the wake of a death, divorce, or other loss. These are all secondary losses that create additional grief that needs to be recognized and mourned.

Another significant secondary loss that can be very profound is the loss of what we will call a "future story." Sally's parents may have had a future story that included a narrative that had her graduate from high school, go to college, get married, and have children of her own—grandchildren for her parents. When a spouse dies, so do the plans, the narratives of what the couple was going to do in retirement or on this year's vacation. With a death, future stories also die or are dramatically altered, resulting in grief over that lost story and that lost future.

People do not always realize that they are possibly mourning these types of secondary losses until some time has passed. It is good for those who spend time with bereaved people to be aware that the person might not understand that some of the depth of the grief they are feeling is related to more than the loss of an individual. It can be helpful to allow them to name some of the other or secondary losses they are mourning. It would not be the role of the caregiver to identify or prescribe what these secondary losses are but rather to encourage the bereaved person to think of and name some of the related losses that might be adding to their grief. Occasionally this can help give a name to some of the grief that can be difficult to identify.

The items mentioned here are by no means an exhaustive list of issues related to the grief of which members of the Bereavement Team need to be aware. There are further resources listed in the bibliography as well as ongoing online education opportunities through organizations such as the Association for Death Education and Counseling, Hospice Foundation of America, and others. Local hospice organizations, grief counseling or support organizations, and funeral homes may also make grief education available to members of the community, especially if they are made aware of the effort being made by a faith community to provide grief support on this level to its members.

CHAPTER 7 — A NEW TABLE

Casseroles, or what are sometimes referred to as one-dish-meals, come by many names and can be found in any cookbook compiled by church or family. Some recipe titles are fortunately descriptive in nature, so you know what you are getting into. Such is the case with these actual prize dishes: *Turkey Crunch Casserole, Corn and Oyster Casserole, Chicken Broccoli Cheese Fettuccini, and Barbeque Lima Beans and Spareribs.* Other dishes have names that are less descriptive, leaving us to wonder just what we are dipping our forks into. These include mysterious things such as *Witches Casserole, Chinese Yap Yap, Emergency Main Dish, and Casserole Delight.* Then there are those that are both descriptive and yet mysterious, such as the *Tuna Unusual Casserole.* Luckily the recipes in these locally created cookbooks generally include the name of the submitter. Most everyone in the church or family knows whose culinary advice and recipes to use and whose should be avoided at all costs.

Whether the casseroles that come after a death are gratefully consumed by a family or hastily and secretly scraped into a garbage can, the casseroles and other food represent caring and acknowledgment that a death has occurred, that there are people who are mourning and hurting, and they need connection, caring, and a community that recognizes their grief. The death rate among humans has been and remains right at 100%. Everything that lives will someday die (cryogenic vats with bodies waiting for reanimation notwithstanding). The sad reality is that anytime a person is loved or has an attachment to another person, there will be grief.

As much as some persons say they want no fuss when they die and do not want to even have their deaths acknowledged, I believe one of the great fears of all humans is to die without anyone to care that we lived and that we died.

The recognition of the grief and the needs of the griever go far beyond what a casserole can provide. Someone loved has been lost, resulting in grief that may or may not be recognized by anyone in the life of the bereaved, especially after the first days or weeks following the death. As the days move on and as friends and others move back into their own busy rhythm of normal existence, life can seem very lonely for those who are still grieving their loss. I have often heard recently bereaved people say that they try not to talk about their loss because they do not want to "burden" others with their sadness and grief. "No one wants to sit there and watch me cry." "No one needs to hear my story again. They have their own lives to live."

Yet, what if a grieving person knew that there were persons, or, better yet, a team of people in their faith community that not only understood their grief and their need to mourn but who were trained and commissioned to walk with them through the silence and the tears? How healing would it be to know there were those who had a ministry of listening, again and again, if necessary, to the story of a long-ago wedding or the tragic description of a death? How refreshing would it be to have someone who understands that they need to hear the name of their deceased loved one, even if it brings them to tears?

> The mention of my child's name
> May bring tears to my eyes,
> But it never fails
> To bring music to my ears.
> If you are really my friend,
> Let me hear the music of her name!
> It soothes my broken heart
> And sings to my soul.
> (Author Unknown)[20]

---

20   James Brooks, *The Unbroken Circle: A Toolkit for Congregations Around Illness, End of Life and Grief,* (Durham, NC: Duke Institute on Care at the End of Life, 2009), p.114.

A team of people who see their ministry as offering a response to those who are grieving brings with it many gifts that are much more healing and supportive than even the best casserole.

THE GIFT OF KNOWLEDGE.

Grieving can be confusing. Minds get a bit muddled for a time, and it is difficult to even understand what we are going through. Some people wonder if they are "doing grief correctly," as if there is some recognized, accepted, and standard way to grieve a significant loss. This ministry team can bring the gift of knowledge about grief to help normalize some of the feelings and reactions the bereaved is experiencing. It can safely be said that this normalization of some of the things a bereaved person is living through can be one of the most helpful gifts that they will receive. This is probably the number one advantage of a grief group. Here a person can sit with others who, although experiencing their own unique grief, also share common emotions, questions, experiences, and things that they find helpful.

THE GIFT OF CONNECTION AND COMMUNITY.

When there has been a death and the casseroles are gone, people drift away. This sometimes includes people nearest the bereaved. It is not uncommon for newly bereaved persons to comment that the people who were close before the death have seemed to drift away. Some of that may be the fear of doing or saying the wrong thing, personal discomfort with death and grief, or the fact that many truly do not understand the needs of the grieving person or family and so feel helpless to know how to best connect. It is also sometimes true that friendships were with another couple or group of couples. A widow or widower may be left out because they or the group do not feel like they fit in any longer. The same can hold true for parents who have lost a child and no longer fit well with their friends whose lives still revolve around children and their activities.

While members of a faith community or the Bereavement Team cannot replace dear friends that seem to fade away, the team member can be a companion that even the most frequent tears cannot chase away and who can possibly draw the person nearer the faith community for extra support and friendship. In reality, when such a connection does happen, a caregiver or faith community member may be bringing much more to the bereaved than just their own presence. When one is experiencing grief or other crises of life, and it seems as if God is silent or far away, God may be right there in the presence, spirit, and love of the people who come to share our pain and sorrow. Who knows? Maybe the Divine can even take the form of a casserole as it is delivered as an offering of kindness and empathy for one's loss.

THE GIFT OF SILENCE

On the other hand, silence can be the most helpful thing when a caregiver is sitting with a person who is mourning a loss. One of the biggest hurdles that grieving people sometimes face is the well-intentioned comments from people who attempt to assist by offering advice or personal experiences with their own grief. Those are generally less than helpful. Normalizing someone's grief is very different from prescribing a solution to that person's grief or trying to generalize our own experience, making it a model of how one should appropriately grieve.

This silence also includes resisting the temptation to share platitudes about grief that are, at best, not helpful and, at worst, actually harmful. "It was God's will," is not helpful to one whose world has been emptied of a dear friend or family member. Avoid the need to say things that are an effort to make someone feel better about their loss. The ability to sit with someone who is grieving and just offer silent support is a tremendous gift.

Silence is especially golden when one needs someone to be with them, hold space with them, and maybe even cry with them.

That silence says more than any words designed to make either the griever or, more often than not, the caregiver, feel better.

There are times when silence is the only thing that can speak to the deepest and most distressing grief. There were multiple times in the hospital when grief literally drove family members to the floor of the room or a hallway. This is grief heavy enough to weigh one down so that sitting on the floor is the only thing to do. In those cases, there was nothing more to do than to just sit on the floor next to them. There are no words that can comfort grief that deep, that weighty, that soul-wrenching. The only communication that can speak to such grief is the silent message that says, "I am here. I will hear your cries. I will bear witness to your pain. When you are able to stand, I will stand with you. When you are ready to talk, I'll be here to listen. But for now, we will sit and let silence have its say."

THE GIFT OF PRESENCE.

As I've already emphasized, you cannot fix grief. It is the natural outgrowth of love, and it will not be fixed. One never stops grieving, although mourning generally ameliorates or eases over time. That is not the same thing as ending grief. What is needed is not a magic potion or incantation to end grief, although many grieving people would wish for such. Since there is not anything that anyone can do to end a person's grief, the greatest gift I know of is the gift of being there for the one who grieves. Nothing in my hands. No plan in mind. No quaint words to make it all better. Just me, my presence, and a depth of caring. Being there to just be present is maybe the most important role for those who would provide support to a bereaved person. There are no simple, nor complex answers for someone who is mourning. It is what it is. The mourner can describe something of how it feels but they cannot make real sense out of it any more than they can make sense out of the death itself. What is needed at this time is presence. A simple assurance that they do not have to be alone in their grief and that there is someone who will be with them as they try to understand that which cannot be understood or explained.

As I transitioned from being a parish pastor into hospital chaplaincy, one of the most difficult lessons for me to learn was that my primary role was to be present. I was not with a patient or family to teach unless I was asked to answer a specific question. I was not there to fix what seemed to me to be broken. I was there to be there, to be present. Sometimes they wished a prayer might be said. Sometimes they wanted someone with whom they could be angry, safely rail against, and maybe even confess. Sometimes they just wanted someone to sit and hold their hand in silence while they cried. Learning to be quiet and just be present for whatever was needed was not an easy lesson but one I learned from the patients and their family members that taught me to just shut up and be present for whatever their need might be.

THE GIFT OF HOPE

There are few more hopeless feelings than watching the death of someone you love. Add to that the sense of frustration of grieving and mourning and wondering if it will ever get better. The simple answer is, yes. With rare exceptions, mourning eases and grief becomes something more bearable to live with. In those early days after a death, however, it is normal to wonder how anything can be better or how you can possibly come to a place where life is something that can be lived without the pain that accompanies the death of someone dear. Recently bereaved people sometimes wonder if there will ever be a normal to their life again.

The short answer is, yes, there will be something normal about life again. It is often referred to as "the new normal" because certainly nothing can be the same as it was before losing a spouse, a parent, or a child. Life changes with the death but it does not always and forever leave a bereaved person stuck in the valley of the shadow of death with no hope and no way out.

Related to the earlier discussion of the loss of the "assumptive world" that occurs when death comes in to upset our lives and our normal, my future may change in an instant. It may seem that my life—my assumptions about my life and future have been shattered. A part of the healing process of the grief experience is the recovery of meaning in one's life. In the literature and research on grief and loss, this is referred to as "meaning-making." It is a recovery phase that results from coping with the reality of what has ended with the death and a hopeful reality as we find a new place for our deceased loved one in our lives. As noted by Thomas Attig, "The central challenge as we grieve is moving from a life where we loved them in presence to a new life where we love them in absence. Nothing is more difficult. Nothing is more important. Nothing is more rewarding."[21]

This recovery or re-orientation of meaning for life may not come quickly or easily. Yet there are things that supporters of the bereaved can do to help them begin to find a hopeful, if very different, future. One of those things is to encourage and listen to their stories and memories. Sometimes people may not always offer memories with all but those who share the same memory. They may fear breaking down and making others feel uncomfortable or may feel that no one else really wants to hear all of their memories of life with the deceased. Given the opportunity and the invitation by a caring listener, however, memories get unraveled. This begins the process of finding a new place in life and heart that the deceased will inhabit as they put their world back in order. Asking to see photos of their life with the deceased is one avenue as is asking them about the legacies their loved one bestowed on them that they will carry with them into the future. These are ways that lives can be opened to find hope and meaning as they journey through life with grief.

---

21 Thomas Attig, "Relearning the World: Making and Finding Meanings," *Meaning Reconstruction and the Experience of Loss*, Robert A. Neimeyer, ed., (Washington, DC: The American Psychological Association, 2010), p. 46.

After the first days following a death have passed, there are no casseroles left uneaten, and no more Jell-O salads are adorning the serving table at the faith community. All of the decadent desserts have been eaten or divided up. The coffee urn is not perking, and the folding metal chairs have been put noisily away. Now, however, there is a new table set for the grief-stricken. It's not a table set with donated plates out of church cupboards and mismatched silverware, but a table set with caring, compassion, and understanding for the needs of those who have suffered a loss. It is a table that welcomes all who grieve. Those who serve at the table are a team of faith community members who offer their nonjudgmental presence, understanding, and compassion.

When word went out that someone in the life of a faith community member had died, the community was hopefully there with love, caring (maybe a casserole or two), and a communal grief to stand beside those most touched by the death. When a ritual was needed to remember and celebrate a person who had lived, was loved, and now had died, the community was there and had its part in that ritual.

Now all of that is over. The body has been buried or cremains have been buried, inurned, or taken home to sit on the mantel in the living room. The world still turns, and life goes on, but grief has come to journey with those who are left to cope with the loss. Who will be there? Who will accompany these mourners on their journey with grief? Is not the faith community, which has been with them through those initial days, the best ally to walk with and escort the grieving person or family through the odyssey ahead of them?

The process that has been suggested here is merely one example of how a faith community might set a new table of support and presence that will feed souls and spirits left hungered by grief. Whether it be an organized effort or something more informal, it is vital that those who would reach out to people who grieve understand the universal, unique, and complex nature of the grief journey. The new table that is to be set for mourners must be a table of faith, understanding, openness, and deep compassion. Those who set the table and then sit with grieving people who come to that table must be people of knowledge, understanding, excellent listening skills, gentleness, and openness to the uniqueness of the human experience. As they companion those of the faith community who grieve, they will be entering into the singular journey of another. These companions will allow the griever to set the pace and lead the way through the unknown terrain before them, trusting that their faith community is there and will be there by their side in faith, through heartache, and to offer courage for their journey. In such a process, healing is possible, and hope is reborn.

Appendix 1 — Bereavement Mailings

Week 1: Condolence card signed by clergy and team members
Week 6:
Week 10:
Week 18:
Week 32:
Week 48:
One Year:
Special Event Mailings
Birthday of Deceased: _____
Birthday of Bereaved: _____
Wedding Anniversary: _____
Christmas: _____

  Other Significant Events: i.e. graduation time, weddings, new baby in the family, any other special events or happenings in the life of the family in which the deceased would play an important role.
Bereavement Follow-Up
Name of Bereaved: _____
Phone: _____
Address: _____
_____
Name of Deceased: _____
Relationship: _____
Date of Death: _____
Date of Funeral or Memorial: _____
Person Assigned to Follow: _____
Phone: _____
2 Weeks: Team Member Visit
Date: _____
Notes:_____
4-5 Weeks: Clergy Visit
Date: _____
Notes:_____
10 Weeks: Team Member Visit

Date: _____

Notes:_____

18 Weeks: Team Member Visit

Date: _____

_____

_____

_____

_____

_____

24 Weeks: Clergy Visit and Assessment

Date: _____

_____

_____

_____

_____

36 Weeks: Team Member Visit

Date: _____

_____

_____

_____

_____

52 Weeks: Clergy Visit

Date: _____

_____

_____

_____

_____

Appendix 2 — Comments to Avoid After a Death

Insensitive Comments

» I know just how you feel. My _____ died last year.
» His/her death was for the best.
» At least you're young enough to remarry/have more children.
» You have to go on with your life.
» Did he/she make peace with God before they died?
» God Clichés
» God needed a small, beautiful flower for his garden.
» God never gives us more than we can handle.
» God must have needed them worse than you did.
» It was a blessing because....
» Now you have an angel in heaven to watch over you.
» Unhealthy Expectations
» You shouldn't act/feel that way.
» You have to be strong for others.
» You have to stay busy.
» You can always find someone worse off than yourself.
» All it takes is a little time and then you'll be fine.

Helpful Phrases After a Death

» I can't imagine how difficult this is for you.
» I'm sorry for your loss.
» My I just sit here with you?
» I know you will miss _____.
» It is harder than most people think.
» It's OK to be angry with God.
» It must be hard to accept.
» What special memories do you have?
» You must have been very close to him/her.

Another thing that is difficult to avoid saying is: "If there is anything I can do, just call." At that early stage the bereaved person doesn't know what they will need, and they probably won't ask, even when they figure it out. It's better to be aware of their situation by observation or through their friends and family and identify something specific you can and would do for them.

» I'd be happy to watch your children while you meet at the funeral home.

» I have an extra bedroom that I'd like to make available for your out-of-town family.

» Since your family is all arriving tomorrow, a couple of us are going to bring dinner to you tomorrow night.

» I'll provide transportation for your family from the airport or back and forth between the church and their motel.

» You've commented that there are some things that you feel need to be done around the house before the family arrives. I'll come over this afternoon and help.

» I'd like to come over and help your children decorate the Christmas tree.

» Here is a box of necessities you will likely need over the next days (paper plates/cups, plastic silverware, paper towels, toilet paper, coffee, etc.).

Appendix 3 — Sharable Items For Bereavement Mailings

Grief Hide and Seek

The church service had just begun, and the congregation and guests were greeting one another. A friend, who knew four of my family members died in 2007, approached me and asked, "How are you?"

"I'm good," I replied. "How are you?"

Widowed a year ago, my friend replied, "Oh, I've found that grief hides. When you think it's gone, you find yourself crying."

I understood her comment. After losing my daughter, father-in-law, brother, and former son-in-law, there have been many times when grief reached out and grabbed me. These moments happen without warning and take me by surprise.

I expect to grieve on my deceased daughter's birthday, and I do. I expect to grieve on the 23rd of the month, the day she died, and I do. I expect to grieve on the anniversary of my father-in-law's death, and brother's death, and I do. But I didn't expect to play hide and seek with grief.

The unpredictable moments of sorrow make me seek the causes. What triggered my grief? Could I have prevented it? Is there more grief work to do? "Grief hides," as my friend put it so clearly, and I've found that it hides in the nooks and crannies of life.

Sometimes, when my granddaughter speaks just like her mother used to, I feel renewed grief. I feel joy as well. When I see someone using a walker, I'm reminded of my father-in law, and I grieve. My brother loved books and I volunteer at the library in his memory. Last week, without any warning, I felt a wave of sadness at his passing.

For someone like me, who has suffered multiple losses, there are many games of hide and seek. Some mourners have a different approach to the game and try to hide or suppress their emotions.

But hiding from emotions only prolongs grief. Thankfully, I've always been honest with my feelings.

If I'm grouchy or feel down, give me an hour, and I can tell you why. As I grow older, I appreciate this personality trait more and more. I also appreciate my ability to identify gut feelings.

Daniel Goleman writes about gut feelings in his book *Emotional Intelligence: Why it can Matter More than IQ.* According to Goleman, being able to identify gut feelings has advantages. This ability gives us the chance to "immediately drop or pursue" different paths with confidence and "pare down our choices."

Nearly four years have passed since my daughter died. Of the four deaths, hers was the most painful. Despite the pain, I have learned from it and one of the things I learned was to accept the hide and seek nature of grief. I accept my feelings and move on. You see, I'm a lucky woman.

My multiple losses reminded me of the miracle of life. So, I'm putting hide and seek nature of grief on notice: You may surprise me, but you will not defeat me. Happiness is mine, to savor each day and to share.

Copyright 2011 by Harriet Hodgson (http://www.harriethodgson.com)

Harriet Hodgson has been an independent journalist for 30+ years. Her 24th book, *Smiling Through Your Tears: Anticipating Grief* written with Lois Krahn, MD, is available from Amazon. Article Source: http://EzineArticles.com/5899608

THE FIRST TIME WE SAID YOUR NAME

The first time we said your name
you broke through the flat crust of your grave
and rose a movable statue,
walking and talking among us.
Since then you've grown a little.
We keep you slightly larger
than life-size, reciting bits of your story,

our favorite odds and ends.
. . . As long as we live, we keep you
from dying your real death,
which is being forgotten. We say,
we don't want to abandon you,
when we mean we can't let you go.
~ Lisa Mueller

POSSIBLE MAILING FOR THE 12TH MONTH AFTER THE DEATH

It has been about a year since you began your journey of grief. Anyone who has suffered a loss has encountered many of the highs and lows of the bereavement process similar to what you have experienced. Some days brought happy and even funny memories while other days brought little more than tears and sadness.

By now you have been through enough to know that there is no right or wrong to any of those experiences. Grief brings what it will bring as it dares us to meet it where we are and sometimes to even "lean into" our grief.

Some people find that the anniversary of a death brings its own special challenges and difficult reminders. At times it is helpful to develop a plan for times such as holidays, anniversaries, birthdays and other special times such as the death anniversary. This month we are sharing a few suggestions that might help you remember and cope in this tender time.

We want you to know that, especially now, your church family is thinking of you, remembering your loved one and, as always, standing ready to offer support where needed.

SUGGESTIONS OF WAYS TO ACKNOWLEDGE THE ANNIVERSARY OF A DEATH

» Visit the person's final resting place.
» Write a letter or a note to your loved one talking about your experience of the past year.

» Write a special tribute or share a special memory on social media.

» Gather some close and supportive friends and share a meal or just a time to sit and trade memories of your loved one and their relationships with her or him.

» Prepare that person's favorite meal to share with family or friends.

» Light a special candle in their memory on the anniversary of the death.

» Listen to some of their favorite music.

» Reach out and do something good for someone in need, a special project or a non-profit in honor of your loved one or volunteer some time to a favorite charity or project.

» Gather and organize family photos, either on your own or with the help of family members.

» Plant a tree, shrub, or flowers in their memory

» Compile a scrapbook of memorabilia.

» Gift something they would have wanted someone to have (books, music, sporting equipment, special photographs, etc.).

» If you are a part of a faith community, consider providing flowers in your loved one's name for a worship service.

» If your faith community has one of those ever-popular "coffee hours" before or after worship, sign up to host one in your loved one's honor.

» Take a drive or trip to a favorite spot or location, either by yourself or as a family.

» Plan to take care of yourself, be gentle with yourself and brave enough to draw others in as you sense a need for support.

A Few Myths About Grief

» All losses are the same.

» All bereaved people grieve the same way.

» When grief is resolved it never comes up again.

» Children grieve like adults.

» Feeling sorry for yourself is not allowable.

» It is better to put painful things out of your mind.

» Expressing feelings that are intense is the same as losing control.

» There is no reason to be angry at your deceased loved one.

» Only sick individuals have physical problems in grief.

» Because you feel crazy, you are going crazy.

» You should feel only sadness that your loved one died.

» Children need to be protected from grief and death.

» Being upset and grieving means that you do not believe in God or trust your religion.

» You and your family will be the same after the death as before your loved one died.

» You will have no relationship with your loved one after the death.

» The intensity and length of your grief are testimony to your love for the deceased.

» Infant death shouldn't be too difficult to resolve because you didn't know the child that well.

» Rituals and funerals are unimportant in helping us deal with life and death in contemporary America.

If Grief Could Speak

If grief could speak it would say, ***I'm sorry***.

I'm sorry it's me that arrived at your doorstep instead of love. But I am made of love too. In fact, it's because I love so much that I hurt so much when I lose the people I love.

If grief could speak it would say, ***You can survive***.

I know you may not want to. I know life may not be worth living without them. I know the earth collapsed beneath your feet. I know a part of you died with them. And I know you can survive, one breath at a time, one moment at a time, one day at a time.

If grief could speak it would say, ***Please don't hide me away***.

I know when people see you with me, they get uncomfortable. I know your friends don't know what to say to me. I know it's easier to hide me away when you have company over for dinner.

But I'd like a seat at the table. Will you let me speak? Will you listen to me? I can't promise I'll be polite or calm. I may raise my voice because I'm angry or I may collapse in a pile of tears, but if I can let it out then I don't have to hold it in here, in you. I'd like to create some more space inside you for all of us to coexist. You, me, love, anger, laughter, peace, hope, joy... there's enough room for all of us in your heart.

If grief could speak it would say, ***I love you***.

You may not love me, but I love you. I love how you love so big. I love how you keep taking care of your babies who lost their papas or their mamas. I love how you keep taking care of that space your loved one took up even though they're gone. How you leave their favorite book in the same place, how you leave their clothes folded, how you let them live a little longer in the things left behind. I love how you don't let the world forget they were here, that they mattered, that they were a part of you. I love you.

If grief could speak it would say, ***Find your own way***.

There seem to be a lot of "experts" out there about me. They say I work in stages, and they make it sound like I'm something to get over, like the flu. What I can tell you is there is nothing wrong with me and there is nothing wrong with you. I am not a sickness, I am grief. I am a valid experience and emotion and there is no right way to hold me. There is just your way. No two people receive me the same way. Let's find our own way to dance together, to cry together, to break together, to heal together.

Let's find our own way through this brief and beautiful life.

Monique Minahan writes about grief, loss and being human. She offers Yoga & Grief classes to bereavement groups. She believes in standing up to live before sitting down to write and listens to her heart to keep her words alive and authentic. Connect with her at monique-minahan.com.

LAMENT PSALM FIVE

O God, find me!
I am lost
In the valley of grief,
and I cannot see my way out.
My friends leave baskets of balm
at my feet, but I cannot bend to touch
the healing
to my heart.
They call me to leave
this valley,
but I cannot follow
the faint sound
of their voices.
They sing their songs
of love,
but the words fade
and vanish in the wind.
They knock,
but I cannot find the door.
They shout to me,
but I cannot find the voice
to answer.
O God, find me!
Come into this valley
and find me!
Bring me out of this land
of weeping.
O you to whom I belong,
find me!
I will wait here,
for you have never failed
to come to me.
I will wait here,

for you have always been faithful.
I will wait here,
for you are my God,
and you have promised
that you counted the hairs on my head.
Ann Weems, *Psalms of Lament,* (Louisville, KY, John Knox Press, 1995, p.9).

WALK WITHIN YOU

~ Taken from Nicholas Evans' book, *The Smoke Jumper*
If I be the first of us to die,
Let grief not blacken long your sky.
Be bold but modest in your grieving.
There is a change but not a leaving.
For just as death is part of life,
The dead live on forever in the living.
And all the gathered riches of our journey,
The moments shared, the mysteries explored,
The steady layering of intimacy stored,
The things that made us laugh or weep or sing,
The joy of sunlit snow or first unfurling of the spring,
The wordless language of look and touch,
The knowing,
Each giving and each taking,
These are not flowers that fade,
Nor trees that fall and crumble,
Nor are they stone,
For even stone cannot the wind and rain withstand
And mighty mountain peaks in time reduce to sand.
What we were, we are.
What we had, we have.
A conjoined past imperishably present.
So when you walk the woods where once we walked together,
And scan in vain the dappled bank beside you for my shadow,

Or pause where we always did upon the hill to gaze across
the land,
> And spotting something, reach by habit for my hand,
> And finding none, feel sorrow start to steal upon you,
> Be still.
> Close your eyes.
> Breathe.
> Listen for my footfall in your heart.
> I am not gone but merely walk within you.

TRICKS YOUR BRAIN PLAYS ON YOU DURING GRIEF

Dr. Bob Baugher, PhD.

Your brain-what an amazing organ. It can outthink the most
complex computer. It is-well-it's who you are. Your brain-or you-is
reading these words and taking in information in microseconds.
So, with all its wondrous abilities, why would your brain trick you,
especially at a time when you need it most? Because it's not perfect.
However, don't let your brain (or you) take it personally. Just keep
reading and you'll begin to recognize how these brain imperfections
can influence you during the most difficult time of your life.

Trick #1: I will feel this way forever.

When the death occurred, you absolutely believed that you
would never laugh again; but you did. Do you remember that first
time? Were you surprised when you heard laughter and realized
that it was coming from you? After you recovered from the shock,
you may have chastised yourself for "forgetting" your loved one.
As time has gone by, however, you have hopefully begun to realize
that your loved one would want laughter to return.

Trick #2: Guilt

Perhaps the cruelest trick your brain plays on you is one where the past continues to be rewritten. Just look at all the ways that guilt can complicate your grief. See if any of these sound familiar:

If-Only Guilt-After the death you find yourself revisiting events in the life of your loved one in which you say, "If only...." Or "I should have....." or "Why didn't I?"

Role Guilt-"I wasn't a good enough _____ to this person." We're still waiting for the perfect (choose one) parent/spouse/sibling/grandparent/child.

Death Causation Guilt-The death occurred because of something I did or failed to do. It matters little whether I actually had anything to do with the death. I still feel guilty.

Trick #3: I'm not like those people who use clichés.

If you're like most bereaved people you've heard so-called words of wisdom and comfort from those folks who think they are somehow helping: Everything happens for a reason, I know just how you feel, and It's time to move one. No doubt these feeble attempts at soothing your pain have caused you some degree of frustration as you say to yourself, "What is wrong with these people? Don't they get it?" However, your brain has deceived you again. Why? Because weren't these some of the same statements you offered to others in grief before you knew better? How quickly our brain "forgets" that we, too, used to be a member of the insensitive crowd.

Trick #4: I need to grieve just right.

This trick is often played on those of us who have issues with perfectionism. The death you've experienced is like no other. Therefore the grief reactions you've been experiencing have thrust you into a world that is foreign to you-into a confusing array of emotions and thoughts swirling around in your brain. As these reactions continue, another part of your brain is asking, "What's wrong with me? Why am I so_____?" Following the death of a loved one you'll never hear someone say, "You know, I'm grieving just right." Instead you hear, "I'm not crying enough." Or "I'm crying too much." Or "I should be more angry." Why these reactions? It's just your struggling brain doing the best it can.

Trick #5: The second year will somehow be easier.

Another trick your brain will play on you is that it will convince you that nothing can be worse than going through each day of the first year-the first birthday, the first holiday, the first Mother's Day or Father's Day, the first Thanksgiving, the first anniversary. All these firsts without our loved one add up to a great deal of pain. For many of us, once the first year is over, our brain conjures yet another deceptive scheme by offering convincing guidance, "Whew! I've made it through one whole year. As difficult as it was, I made it through each day. Year two should be better." Better? Well, maybe for some people. But if you are like many people, you discovered that your brain lied. You found that, in some ways the second year was more difficult. Why? Because much of the first-year shock had worn off and now the pain is raw.

Trick #6: My grief is worse than anyone else's.

At first, as you came across other people who had a loss different from yours it may have been easy for your brain to come up with the belief that went something like this: "Yes, these people are also in pain. But their loss is not like mine. Their pain cannot be as intense, as deep, and long lasting as mine." When you began to meet people who had a similar loss, your brain may have concluded, "Their loss is terrible, but they must not have loved their person as much as I love mine." Later, as you look back, you may have realized that the pain you were going through made it difficult to really feel the depth of grief and despair experienced by others as they coped with their own loss. You now realize that, while you can never measure the amount of another's pain, you have come to understand that, in our humanness, we are all united by our grief because it demonstrates that we all have loved.

Trick #7: Relatives who haven't spoken to one another will put aside their differences because of this death.

When the death hit you and your family, your brain might have concluded, "The tragedy and finality of this death in our family will surely bring people together. Family members will awaken to the fact that life is too short to hold grudges, to persist in silent indifference to the feelings of others, and to withhold forgiveness." However, you have sadly realized again that your brain was wrong.

Trick #8: I will get a little better each day.

In the past, when other negative events occurred in your life, you may have found that, day after day, things did get a little better. In the case of grief, you almost cannot blame your brain for coming up with a similar belief. However, you may have discovered that day 90 following the death was worse than day 30 and that you may have felt worse at the ten month point than you did at the five-month point. Why is this? One reason is shock, which is your brain's way of cushioning the intensity of the blow. Whether death is sudden or expected, our brain goes into shock for a period of time. The length is different for everyone. As you know, when shock begins to wear off, the pain begins to set in. This is one of the major reasons that, when people look back on the weeks and months following a death, they report that it was like they were in a fog, like they were going through the motions much like a robot. People use terms like, "I was on automatic pilot." Or "I was a zombie." Shock is your brain trying to protect itself (you) from the full impact of the pain.

Trick #9: Letting go of my grief means letting go of my loved one.

This brain maneuver is one of the biggest challenges in coping with grief. If you could actually hear your brain speaking to you, the words would sound something like this: "Now that some time has gone by I can feel that the intensity of my loss easing up just a little. But wait! I can't let this happen because if the pain begins to leave, the memories of my loved one will slip away as well. So, I must hold on to my sorrow, heartache, and anguish in order to preserve the connection with this person." This brain tactic is related to a type of guilt called, Moving On Guilt in which guilt feelings surface at the moment the bereaved person begins to feel a little better. As you know, an important part of your grief work is to hold on to the memories while simultaneously letting the pain of the loss gradually subside.

So, there they are: ten tricks of the brain that complicate the bereavement process. Some you knew already and found yourself nodding your head. A couple of them may have been new to you as you have come to realize that the death of your loved one has challenged your brain in ways it has never experienced before. In considering these tricks, you will now hopefully be a little kinder to your brain as it continues to cope with the loss of someone you love.

Dr. Bob Baugher is a Psychology Instructor at Highline Community College in Des Moines, Washington, where he teaches courses in Suicide Intervention, Death & Life, Psychology of Human Relations, Understanding AIDS, and Abnormal Psychology. Bob has given more than 500 workshops on grief and loss.

"WHO AM I?" TEST

Robert A. Neimeyer

Begin by writing down four responses to the question: "Who was I before my husband died?" The answers might focus on your beliefs, values, characteristics, things you did, or people who were important to you. For example, you might say you believed in working hard to get ahead, valued caring for others, was a runner and regularly spent time with family and friends. Then repeat the exercise focusing on the questions "Who am I now?" and "Who do I want to be in the future?" This can help us reconnect with core, enduring purposes in our lives, to find strands of consistency, and also consider what needs to receive more attention for us to find a way back to a life and identity that have meaning for us.

BIBLIOGRAPHY AND RESOURCES

Attig, Thomas. "Relearning the World: Making and Finding Meanings." *Meaning Reconstruction and the Experience of Loss.* Edited by Robert A. Neimeyer. Washington, DC: The American Psychological Association, 2010.

Corr, Charles A., Clyde M. Nabe, and Donna M. Corr, *Death and Dying: Life and Living,* 4th edition. Belmont, CA: Wadsworth/Thomson Learning.

DeSpelder, Lynne Ann and Albert Lee Strickland. *The Last Dance: Encountering Death and Dying,* 7th edition. New York, NY: McGraw Hill, 1998.

DeSpelder, Lynne Ann and Strickland, Albert Lee. The Last Dance: Encountering Death and Dying. 7th edition. New York, NY: McGraw Hill, 2005.

Devine, Megan. *It's OK That You're Not OK: Meeting Grief and Loss in a Culture That Doesn't Understand.* Boulder, CO, Sounds True, 2017.

Doka, Kenneth and Terry Martin, *Grieving Beyond Gender: Understanding the Ways Men and Women Grieve,* Revised Edition. New York, NY: Routledge, 2010.

Doka, Kenneth, Editor. *Disenfranchised Grief: New Directions, Challenges and Strategies for Practice.* Champaign, IL, Research Press, 2002.

Doka, Kenneth. "The Spiritual Crisis of Bereavement," In *Death and Spirituality.* Kenneth Doka, Editor. Amityville, NY, Baywood Publishing, 1993.

Houptman, Judith. "Death and Mourning: A Time for Weeping, A Time for Healing." *Death and Bereavement Around the World,* Vol. 1. John D. Morgan and Pittu Laungani, Editors. Amityville, NY: Baywood Publishing, 2002.

Kubler-Ross, Elizabeth. *On Death and Dying.* New York, NY: The MacMillan Co., 1969.

Landsman, Irene. "Crisis of Meaning in Trauma and Loss." In *Loss of the Assumptive World: A Theory of Traumatic Loss.* Jeffrey Kauffman, editor. New York, NY: Brunner-Routledge, 2002.

Mitchell, Kenneth and Anderson, Herbert. *All Our Losses All Our Griefs: Resources for Pastoral Care.* Louisville, KY: Westminster John Knox Press, 1983.

Norris, Kaye, Gretchen Strohmaier, Charles Asp, and Iras Byock. "Spiritual Care at the End of Life." *Health Progress.* July-August 2004.

Roberts, Barbara. *Death Without Denial Grief Without Apology: A Guide for Facing Death and Loss.* Troutdale, OR: New Sage Press, Troutdale, OR 2002.

Stroebe, Margaret and Henk Schut. "The Dual Model of Coping with Bereavement: Rationale and Description." *Death Studies*, 23:3 (1999): 197-224.

Worden, William. *Grief Counseling and Grief Therapy,* 3rd edition. New York, NY: Springer Publishing Co. 1991.

Other Helpful Resources

Brooks, James L. *The Unbroken Circle: A Toolkit for Congregations Around Illness, End of Life and Grief.* Durham, NC: Duke Institute on End-of-Life Care, 2009.

Elison, Jennifer and Chris McGonigle. *Liberating Losses: When Death Brings Relief.* Cambridge, MA: Da Capo Lifelong Books, 2004.

Hughes, Marylou. *Bereavement and Support: Healing in a Group Environment.* Philadelphia, PA: Taylor and Francis Publishing, 1995.

Kauffman, Jeffrey, Editor. *The Shame of Death, Grief, and Trauma.* New York, NY: Routledge, 2010.

Lester, Andrew, D. *Hope In Pastoral Care and Counseling.* Louisville, KY: Westminster John Knox Press, 1995.

Neimeyer, Robert A., Editor. *Meaning Reconstruction and the Experience of Loss.* Washington, DC The American Psychological Association, 2010.

Neimeyer, Robert A., et al. Editors. *Grief and Bereavement in Contemporary Society: Bridging Research and Practice.* New York, NY: Routledge, 2011.

Smith, Harold Ivan. *When Your People Are Grieving: Leading in Times of Loss.* Kansas City, MO, Beacon Hill Press, 2001.

****

I highly recommend the website, aftertalk.com. It is free to subscribe. Check out their website.

Excellent resources are also available through the Hospice Foundation of America at hospicefoundation.org. They have very helpful online training opportunities and other resources that are made available.

Compassionatefriends.org —Compassionate Friends is an international organization with local chapters in many cities. They support parents who have lost a child of any age.

Additional research is being written and published in the area of end of life and bereavement all of the time and there are many online resources that can be cautiously considered.

Dan Dixson is available to lead workshops or retreats on topics related to end-of- life and bereavement for faith communities, healthcare and hospice professionals or regional gatherings.

CPSIA information can be obtained
at www.ICGtesting.com
Printed in the USA
BVHW071242130423
662286BV00007B/473

9 781631 998645